Contents

Foreword

I've been a React developer since its inception. When I first encountered it, there was an air of mystery surrounding it as it distinguished itself from its competitors by emphasizing the exclusive use of components. Over a decade later, I find myself unable to envision working with any other framework in the near future. React continues to reinvent itself while pushing other frameworks around it to evolve too. As a freelance web developer collaborating closely with companies, React is my indispensable daily companion, enhancing my productivity in every project.

"The Road to React" made its debut in 2016, and since then, I've almost rewritten it annually. This book teaches the core principles of React, guiding you through building a practical application in pure React without complex tooling. The book covers everything from setting up the project to deploying it on a server. Each chapter includes additional recommended reading and exercises. By the end, you'll have the skills to develop your own React applications.

In "The Road to React," I establish a solid foundation before delving into the broader React ecosystem. The book clarifies general concepts, patterns, and best practices for real-world React applications. Ultimately, you'll learn to construct a React application from scratch, incorporating features such as pagination, client-side and server-side searching, and advanced UI interactions like sorting. My aspiration is that this book conveys my passion for React and JavaScript, helping you embark on your journey with confidence.

About the Author

I am a German software and web developer with a passion for learning and teaching JavaScript. Following the completion of my Master's Degree in computer science, I immersed myself in the startup world, extensively using JavaScript both professionally and in my free time. Collaborating with an exceptional team of engineers in Berlin, we developed large-scale JavaScript applications which sparked my interest in sharing this knowledge with others.

During this time, I regularly authored articles on web development for my website. Positive feedback from readers seeking to learn from my articles motivated me to refine my writing and teaching style. With each article, my ability to effectively educate others continued to grow. Witnessing students thrive by providing them with clear objectives and quick feedback loops is particularly fulfilling.

Presently, I operate as a self-employed web developer, closely working with companies on their products. More information about collaborating with me can be found on my website[1].

---

[1]https://www.robinwieruch.de/

FAQ

How to get updates?

Stay informed about the latest updates through two channels. You can subscribe to email updates[2] or follow me on Twitter[3]. Regardless of the channel you choose, rest assured that I prioritize sharing only high-quality content. Upon receiving a notification about an update for the book, simply visit my website to download the latest version of the book.

Is the learning material up-to-date?

Unlike traditional programming books that quickly become outdated, this self-published book allows for prompt updates whenever new versions of relevant tools or technologies are released. Rest assured, you'll always have access to the latest information.

Can I get a digital copy of the book if I've purchased it on Amazon?

If you've purchased the book on Amazon, you might have noticed it's also available on my website. Since I use Amazon as one way to generate revenue for my frequently free content, I genuinely appreciate your support and I encourage you to sign up for my courses[4]. Once you've created an account, send me an email detailing your Amazon purchase. This will enable me to unlock the content for you. By having an account on my platform, you'll always enjoy access to the most up-to-date version of the book. Thank you for your support!

Why is the print version so large?

If you've acquired the print version of the book, consider making notes directly in its pages. The deliberate choice to keep the printed book extra-large was made to provide ample space for extensive code snippets and to afford you sufficient room for your annotations and personal notes. This size decision was crafted with the intention of enhancing your overall reading and learning experience.

Why does the book not have many pages?

The print version's larger dimensions contribute to fewer pages. While most sections are concise, detailed material is available online for in-depth insights. This allows a smooth reading experience, with essential React concepts covered in the book for a quick start. Engaging in optional exercises is encouraged for a comprehensive understanding.

Why is the book written like a long read tutorial?

The unconventional manner in which this book is written and structured might come as a surprise to those more accustomed to the conventional format of programming texts. When I first started coding, there was a scarcity of practical, hands-on resources available. As a learner, I found great value in materials that provided step-by-step instructions, guiding me through not only the 'what' and 'how' but also the 'why' behind each concept. With the goal of replicating this immersive learning

---

[2]https://rwieruch.substack.com/
[3]https://twitter.com/rwieruch
[4]https://courses.robinwieruch.de/

experience, I've taken on the task of self-publishing, hoping to extend this valuable knowledge-sharing opportunity to fellow developers within our community.

What do I do if I encounter a bug?

Should you come across any bugs in the code, locate the current GitHub project URL at the end of each section. Feel free to open a GitHub issue there, and your assistance will be highly valued!

Who is this book for?

JavaScript Beginners

JavaScript beginners with knowledge in fundamental JS, CSS, and HTML: If you just started out with web development, and have a basic grasp of JS, CSS, and HTML, this book should give you everything that's needed to learn React. However, if you feel there is a gap in your JavaScript knowledge, don't hesitate to read up on that topic before continuing with the book. You will have lots of references to fundamental JavaScript knowledge in this book though.

JavaScript Veterans

JavaScript veterans coming from jQuery: If you have used JavaScript with jQuery, MooTools, and Dojo extensively back in the days, the new JavaScript era may seem overwhelming for someone getting back on track with it. However, most of the fundamental knowledge didn't change, it's still JavaScript and HTML under the hood, so this book should give you the right start into React.

JavaScript Enthusiasts

JavaScript enthusiasts with knowledge in other modern SPA frameworks: If you are coming from Angular or Vue, there may be lots of differences in how to write applications with React, however, all these frameworks share the same fundamentals of JavaScript and HTML. After a mindset shift to get comfortable with React, you should be doing just fine adopting React.

Non-JavaScript Developers

If you are coming from another programming language, you should be more familiar than others with the different aspects of programming. After picking up the fundamentals of JavaScript and HTML, you should have a good time learning React with me.

Designers and UI/UX Enthusiasts

If your main profession is in design, user interaction, or user experience, don't hesitate to pick up this book. You may be already quite familiar with HTML and CSS which is a plus. After going through some more JavaScript fundamentals, you should be good to get through this book. These days UI/UX is moving closer to the implementation details which are often taken care of with React. It would be your perfect asset to know how things work in code.

Team Leads, Product Owners, or Product Managers

If you are a team lead, product owner or product manager of your development department, this book should give you a good breakdown of all the essential parts of a React application. Every section explains one React concept/pattern/technique to add another feature or to improve the overall architecture. It's a well-rounded reference guide for React.

How to read the book?

Most programming books are high-level and go into very much technical detail, but they lack the ability to get their readers into coding. That's why this book may be different from the books that you are used to reading in this domain, because it attempts to teach aspiring developers actual programming. Hence I try to keep a good balance between being pragmatic, by giving you all the tools to get the job done, while still being detail-oriented, by giving you as much information as needed to understand these tools and how they are used in practice.

Every section in this book introduces you to a new topic. For the fast pace learners who do not want to go into much detail, it's possible to read from section to section. However, if learners want to dive deeper into certain topics, they can read more by following the footnotes. I want to offer you a way to get a great overview of the topic at hand while still enabling you to dig deeper if you want to. After reading the book either way, you should be able to code what you have learned in a pragmatic way.

Take Notes

If you have a print version of the book, do not hesitate to underline paragraphs, to write notes, or to annotate code snippets. That's why it has such a large size in the first place. If you don't have a print version, keep a notebook on the side for your learnings. Taking notes fortifies what you have learned and you can always come back to them. With every new learning, you will get a better understanding of the big picture and how the smaller pieces fit together, so it's a great exercise on the side to write down your learnings on a piece of paper.

Code Code Code

Every section introduces you to a new topic in a pragmatic way. For this reason just reading through the section does not suffice to become a developer, because there is lots of things going on in one section alone. So you shouldn't rush from section to section, but instead I recommend you to have a computer by your side which allows you to code along the way.

Do not just copy paste code, instead type it yourself. Do not be satisfied when you just used the code from the book, instead experiment with it. See what breaks the code and how to fix it. See how certain changes affect the result. And see how you can extend or even improve the code by adding a few lines to it. That's what coding is all about after all. It does not help you to rush through the book if you haven't written a line of code once. So get your hands dirty and do more coding than reading!

Anticipate

There will be many coding problems presented in this book. Often I will give you the option to solve things yourself before reading about the solution in the next paragraph or code snippet. However, it breaks the flow of repeating myself, so I keep these encouragements to a minimum. Instead I am hoping for your eagerness here to jump ahead. Try to solve things before I get the chance to present you the solution. Only by trying, failing, and solving a problem you will become a better developer.

Take Breaks

Since every section introduces you to a new topic, it happens fast that you forget the learnings from the previous section. In addition to coding along with every section, I recommend you to take breaks between the sections which allow the learnings to sink in. Read the section, code along the way, do the exercise afterwards, code even a bit more if you like, and then rest. Think about your learnings while taking a walk outside or speak with someone about what you have learned even though this other person is not into coding. After all, taking breaks is always essential if you want to learn something new.

Fundamentals of React

In the initial phase of this learning journey, we'll delve into the essential foundations of React, guiding you through the creation of your first React project. As we progress, we'll expand our exploration of React's capabilities, implementing practical features such as client and server-side searching, remote data fetching, and advanced state management. This hands-on approach mirrors the development of a real-world web application. By the end, you'll have a fully functional React application seamlessly interacting with real-world data.

Hello React

Single-page applications (SPA[5]) have become increasingly popular with first-generation SPA frameworks like Angular (by Google), Ember, Knockout, and Backbone. Using these frameworks made it easier to build web applications that advanced beyond vanilla JavaScript and jQuery. React, introduced by Facebook in 2013, is another solution for SPAs, offering yet another powerful framework for building modern web applications in JavaScript.

Let's take a trip back in time before the advent of SPAs: In the past, websites and web applications were server-rendered. When a user accessed a URL in a browser, a request was made to a web server, fetching one HTML file along with its associated HTML, CSS, and JavaScript files. After some network delay, the user would see the rendered HTML in the browser and could begin interacting with it. Each subsequent page transition would trigger this sequence of events again. In this earlier version, the server handled most essential tasks, while the client's role was minimal, primarily focused on rendering pages. Basic HTML and CSS structured and styled the application, with a touch of JavaScript, often in the form of the popular library jQuery, to enable interactions (e.g. toggling a dropdown) or advanced styling (e.g. positioning a tooltip).

In contrast, SPA frameworks shifted the focus from the server to the client. In the world of SPAs, the server primarily delivers JavaScript over the network, accompanied by a minimal HTML file. The HTML file then executes the linked JavaScript files on the client-side (browser) to render the entire application using HTML (and CSS), while still relying on JavaScript for interactions. In its most extreme manifestation, a user visiting a URL requests a small HTML file and a larger JavaScript file. Following a network and rendering delay, the user sees the HTML rendered by JavaScript in the browser. Subsequent page transitions do not necessitate additional file requests from the web server but instead utilize the initially requested JavaScript to render new pages.

React, along with other SPA solutions, played a pivotal role in making this transformation possible. Essentially, a SPA is a single, organized bundle of JavaScript, neatly structured into folders and files, creating an entire application. The SPA framework, such as React, provides the necessary tools to architect this JavaScript-focused application. When a user visits the URL for your web application, this JavaScript-centric application is delivered once over the network to their browser. Subsequently, React or any other SPA framework takes charge of rendering everything in the browser as HTML and managing user interactions with JavaScript.

With the ascent of React, the concept of components gained popularity. Each component defines its visual and functional aspects using HTML, CSS, and JavaScript. Once a component is established, it can be integrated into a hierarchy of components to construct a complete application. While React primarily focuses on components as a library, its adaptable ecosystem positions it as a flexible framework. Featuring a streamlined API, a flourishing yet stable ecosystem, and a supportive community, React is ready to welcome you with open arms! :-)

---

[5]https://bit.ly/3BZOL1o

Exercises

- Read more about Websites and Web Applications[6].
- Watch React.js: The Documentary[7].
- Read more about JavaScript fundamentals needed for React[8].
- Optionally, if you need a motivational boost:
  - Read more about how to learn a framework[9].
  - Read more about how to learn React[10].
- Optional: Leave feedback for this section[11].

---

[6]https://www.robinwieruch.de/web-applications/

[7]https://bit.ly/3xrvxkI

[8]https://www.robinwieruch.de/javascript-fundamentals-react-requirements/

[9]https://www.robinwieruch.de/how-to-learn-framework/

[10]https://www.robinwieruch.de/learn-react-js/

[11]https://forms.gle/NTqhvyDaP1RjtanC6

Requirements

To navigate through this book, it's essential to have a foundational understanding of web development, encompassing HTML, CSS, and JavaScript. Familiarity with APIs[12] is beneficial, as they will be discussed later. Additionally, you'll require the following coding tools to follow along with the book, complementing these skills.

Editor and Terminal

For this learning experience, you will need an editor (e.g. Sublime Text) and a command line tool (e.g. iTerm). As an alternative, I recommend using an IDE, for example **Visual Studio Code** (also called VSCode), for beginners, as it's an all-in-one solution that provides an advanced editor with an integrated command line tool, and because it is the most popular choice among web developers. I have provided a setup guide[13] to get you started with general web development. It comes with all the details and I keep it separate from the book, because it offers options for Windows and MacOS users.

If you don't want to set up the editor/terminal combination or IDE on your local machine, **CodeSandbox**[14], an online editor, is also a viable alternative. While CodeSandbox is a great tool for sharing code online, a local machine setup is a better tool for learning the different ways to create a web application. Also, if you want to develop applications professionally, a local setup will be required.

Throughout this learning experience, I will use the term *command line*, which will be used synonymously for the terms *command line tool*, *terminal*, and *integrated terminal*. The same applies to the terms *editor*, *text editor*, and *IDE*, depending on what you decided to use for your setup.

Optionally, I recommend managing projects on **GitHub** while we conduct the exercises in this book, and I've provided a short guide[15] on how to use these tools. Github has excellent version control, so you can see what changes were made if you make a mistake or just want a more direct way to follow along. It's also a great way to share your code later with other people.

Node and NPM

Before we can begin, we'll need to have **Node and NPM**[16] installed. Both are used to manage libraries (node packages) that you will need along the way. These node packages can be libraries or whole frameworks. We'll install external node packages via npm (node package manager).

You can verify node and npm versions on the command line using the `node --version` and `npm --version` commands. If you don't receive output in the terminal indicating which version is installed, you need to install node and npm:

---

[12]https://www.robinwieruch.de/what-is-an-api-javascript/
[13]https://www.robinwieruch.de/developer-setup/
[14]https://codesandbox.io
[15]https://www.robinwieruch.de/git-essential-commands/
[16]https://nodejs.org/en/

Command Line

```
node --version
*vXX.YY.ZZ
npm --version
*vXX.YY.ZZ
```

If you have already installed Node and npm, make sure that your installation is the most recent version. If you're new to npm or need a refresher, this npm crash course[17] I created will get you up to speed.

Exercises:

- Optional: Read more about yarn[18] and pnpm[19]. Both can be used as a replacement for npm. However, I do not recommend using them as a beginner. This exercise should only make sure that you know about the alternatives.

---

[17]https://www.robinwieruch.de/npm-crash-course/
[18]https://yarnpkg.com/
[19]https://pnpm.io/

Setting up a React Project

In the Road to React, we'll use Vite[20] to set up our React application. Vite, a french word which translates to "quick", is a modern build tool for status quo web frameworks (e.g. React) which comes with sensible defaults (read: configuration) while staying highly extensible for specific use cases (e.g. SVGs, Linting, TypeScript). The essential core of Vite is a **development server**, which allows you to start your React application on your local machine (read: development environment), and a bundler, which outputs highly optimized files for a production-ready deployment (read: production environment). What matters for a React beginner here: getting started with React by just learning React while not getting distracted by any tooling around it. Therefore Vite is the perfect partner for learning React.

There are two ways to create your project with Vite. First, choosing an online template[21], either React (recommended for this book) or React TypeScript (advanced, which means you implement the types for TypeScript yourself) for working on your project online without a local setup. Second, which is the way I would recommend, is creating a React project with Vite on your local machine for working on it in your local IDE (e.g. VSCode).

Since the online template works out of the box, we will focus on the setup for your local machine in this section (recommended). In a previous section, you have installed Node and npm. The latter enables you to install third-party dependencies (read: libraries, frameworks, etc.) from the command line. So open up your command line tool and move to a folder where you want to create your React project. As a crash course for navigating on the command line:

- use pwd (on Windows: cd) to display the current folder
- use ls (on Windows: dir) to display all folders and files in the current folder
- use mkdir <folder_name> to create a folder
- use cd <folder_name> to move into a folder
- use cd .. to move outside of a folder

After navigating into a folder where you want to create your React project, type the following command. We'll refer to this project as *hacker-stories*, but you may choose any project name you like:

Command Line

```
npm create vite@latest hacker-stories -- --template react
```

Optionally you can also go with a React + TypeScript project if you feel confident (check Vite's installation website to follow their instructions for a React + TypeScript project). The book comes with a TypeScript section later, however, it will not do any hand-holding throughout the sections for

---
[20]https://bit.ly/3BsG1TH
[21]https://bit.ly/3RPAZWz

transforming JavaScript into TypeScript. Only at the end of each section you will find an alternative TypeScript implementation.

Next, follow the instructions given on the command line for navigating into the folder, installing all the third-party dependencies of the project, and running it locally on your machine:

Command Line

```
cd hacker-stories
npm install
npm run dev
```

The command line should output a URL where you can find your project running in the browser. Open up the browser with the given URL and verify that you can see the React project running there. We will continue developing this project in the next sections, however, for the rest of this section, we will go through explaining the project structure and the scripts (e.g. npm run dev).

Project Structure

First, let's open the application in an editor/IDE. For VSCode, you can simply type `code` . on the command line. The following folder structure, or a variation of it depending on the *Vite* version, should be presented:

Project Structure

```
hacker-stories/
--node_modules/
--public/
----vite.svg
--src/
----assets/
------react.svg
----App.css
----App.jsx
----index.css
----main.jsx
--.eslintrc.cjs
--.gitignore
--index.html
--package-lock.json
--package.json
--README.md
--vite.config.js
```

This is a breakdown of the most important folders and files:

- **package.json:** This file shows you a list of all third-party dependencies (read: node packages which are located in the *node_modules/* folder) and other essential project configurations related to Node/npm.
- **package-lock.json:** This file indicates npm how to break down (read: resolve) all node package versions and their internal third-party dependencies. We'll not touch this file.
- **node_modules/:** This folder contains all node packages that have been installed. Since we used Vite to create our React application, there are various node modules (e.g. React) already installed for us. We'll not touch this folder.
- **.gitignore:** This file indicates all folders and files that shouldn't be added to your git repository when using git, as such files and folders should be located only on your local machine. The *node_modules/* folder is one example. It is enough to share the *package.json* and *package-lock.json* files with other developers in the team, so they can install dependencies on their end with `npm install` without having to share the entire *node_modules/* folder with everybody.

- **vite.config.js**: A file to configure Vite. If you open it, you should see Vite's React plugin showing up there. If you would be running Vite with another web framework, the other framework's Vite plugin would show up. In the end, there are many more things that can optionally be set up here.
- **public/**: This folder holds static assets for the project like a favicon[22] which is used for the browser tab's thumbnail when starting the development server or building the project for production.
- **index.html**: The HTML that is displayed in the browser when starting the project. If you open it, you shouldn't see much content though. However, you should see a script tag which links to your source folder where all the React code is located to output HTML/CSS in the browser.

In the beginning, everything you need is located in the *src/* folder. The main focus lies on the *src/App.jsx* file which is used to implement React components. It will be used to implement your application, but later you might want to split up your React components into multiple files, where each file maintains one or more components on its own. We will arrive at this point eventually.

Additionally, you will find a *src/main.jsx* as an entry point to the React world. You will get to know this file in later sections. There is also a *src/index.css* and a *src/App.css* file to style your overall application and components, which comes with the default style when you open them. You will modify them later as well.

---

[22]https://bit.ly/3QvRupG

npm Scripts

After you have learned about the folder and file structure of your React project, let's go through the available commands. All your project-specific commands can be found in your *package.json* file under the `scripts` property. They may look similar to these depending on your Vite version:

package.json

```
"dev": "vite",
"build": "vite build",
"lint": "eslint . --ext js,jsx --report-unused-disable-directives --max-warnings 0",
"preview": "vite preview"
```

These scripts are executed with the `npm run <script>` command in an IDE-integrated terminal or your standalone command line tool. The commands are as follows:

Command Line

```
# Runs the application locally for the browser
npm run dev


# Lint the application locally for code style errors
npm run lint


# Builds the application for production
npm run build
```

Another command from the previous npm scripts called `preview` can be used to run the production-ready build on your local machine for testing purposes. In order to make it work, you have to execute `npm run build` before running `npm run preview`. Essentially `npm run dev` and `npm run preview` (after `npm run build`) should give the identical output in the browser. However, the former is not optimized for production and should exclusively be used for the local development of the application.

Exercises:

- Read more about Vite[23].
- Exercise npm scripts:
    - Start your React application with `npm run dev` on the command line and check it out in the browser.
        * Exit the command on the command line by pressing `Control + C`.

---

[23]https://bit.ly/3BsG1TH

– Run the `npm run build` script and verify that a *dist/* folder was added to your project. Note that the build folder can be used later on to deploy your application. Afterward, run `npm run preview` to see the production-ready application in the browser.

- Every time we change something in our source code throughout the coming sections, make sure to check the output in your browser for getting visual feedback. Use `npm run dev` to keep your application running.
- Optional: If you use git and GitHub, add and commit your changes after every section of the book.
- Optional: Leave feedback for this section[24].

---

[24]https://forms.gle/bvH2jcppsSA6p9i16

Meet the React Component

Every React application is built on the foundation of **React components**. In this section, you will get to know your first React component which is located in the *src/App.jsx* file and which should look similar to the example below. Depending on your Vite version, the content of the file might differ slightly:

src/App.jsx

```jsx
import { useState } from 'react';
import reactLogo from './assets/react.svg';
import viteLogo from '/vite.svg';
import './App.css';

function App() {
  const [count, setCount] = useState(0);

  return (
    <>
      <div>
        <a href="https://vitejs.dev" target="_blank" rel="noreferrer">
          <img src={viteLogo} className="logo" alt="Vite logo" />
        </a>
        <a href="https://react.dev" target="_blank" rel="noreferrer">
          <img
            src={reactLogo}
            className="logo react"
            alt="React logo"
          />
        </a>
      </div>
      <h1>Vite + React</h1>
      <div className="card">
        <button onClick={() => setCount((count) => count + 1)}>
          count is {count}
        </button>
        <p>
          Edit <code>src/App.jsx</code> and save to test HMR
        </p>
      </div>
      <p className="read-the-docs">
        Click on the Vite and React logos to learn more
      </p>
```

```
      </>
   );
}
```

```
export default App;
```

This file will be our focus throughout this book, unless otherwise specified. Even though this file will grow in size, because we are not splitting it up from the beginning into multiple files, it will be simpler to understand as a beginner, because everything is at one place. Once you get more comfortable with React, I will show you how to split your React project with your components into multiple files.

Let's start by reducing this React component to a more lightweight version for getting you started without too much distracting boilerplate code[25]:

src/App.jsx

```
function App() {
  return (
    <div>
      <h1>Hello React</h1>
    </div>
  );
}
```

```
export default App;
```

Optionally I recommend making the *src/index.css* and *src/App.css* files blank for starting from a clean slate style-wise. Next, start your application with npm run dev on the command line and check what's displayed in the browser. You should see the headline "Hello React" showing up. Before we dive deeper into each topic, here comes a quick overview of what's in your code and what we will cover more in-depth in the following sections:

- First, this React component, specifically called App component, is just a JavaScript function. In contrast to traditional JavaScript functions, it's defined in PascalCase[26]. A component has to start with a capital letter, otherwise it isn't treated as a component in React. The kind of the App component is commonly called a **function component**. Function components are the modern way of using components in React, however, be aware that there are other variations of React components (see **component types** in a later section) too.
- Second, the App component doesn't have any parameters in its function signature yet. In the upcoming sections, you will learn how to pass information (see **props** in a later section) from one component to another component. These props will be accessible via the function's signature as parameters then.

---

[25]https://bit.ly/3lZzckS
[26]https://www.robinwieruch.de/javascript-naming-conventions/

- And third, the App component returns code that resembles HTML. You will see how this new syntax (see **JSX** in a later section), allows you to combine JavaScript and HTML for displaying highly dynamic and interactive content in a browser.

Like any other JavaScript function, a function component can have implementation details between the function signature and the return statement. You will see this in practice in action throughout your React journey:

src/App.jsx

```
function App() {
  // you can do something in between

  return (
    <div>
      <h1>Hello React</h1>
    </div>
  );
}

export default App;
```

Variables defined in the function's body will be re-defined each time this function runs, which shouldn't be something new if you are familiar with JavaScript and its functions:

src/App.jsx

```
function App() {
  const title = 'React';

  return (
    <div>
      <h1>Hello React</h1>
    </div>
  );
}

export default App;
```

The function of a component runs every time a component is displayed in the browser. This happens for the initial displaying (read: rendering) of the component, but also whenever the component updates because it has to display something different due to changes (re-rendering). We will learn more about this later too.

Since we do not want to re-define a variable within a function every time this function runs, we could define this variable outside of the component as well. In this case, the title does not depend on any information that's within the function component (e.g. parameters coming from the function's signature), hence it's okay to move it outside. Therefore it will be defined only once and not every time the function is called:

src/App.jsx

```
const title = 'React';

function App() {
  return (
    <div>
      <h1>Hello React</h1>
    </div>
  );
}

export default App;
```

On your journey as a React developer, and in this learning experience, you will come across both scenarios: variables (and functions) defined outside and within a component. As a rule of thumb: If a variable does not need anything from within the function component's body (e.g. parameters), then define it outside of the component which avoids re-defining it on every function call.

Exercises:

- Compare your source code against the author's source code[27].
    - Optional: If you are using TypeScript, check out the author's source code here[28].
- Think about ways to display the title variable in your App component's returned HTML. In the next section, we'll put this variable to use.
- Optional: Leave feedback for this section[29].

---

[27]https://bit.ly/490FAxX
[28]https://bit.ly/3OvfqLO
[29]https://forms.gle/VYiZqqjzXGE11wCv6

React JSX

Everything returned from a React component will be displayed in the browser. Until now, we only returned HTML from the App component. However, recall that I mentioned the returned output of the App component not only resembles HTML, but it can also be mixed with JavaScript. In fact, this output is called **JSX (JavaScript XML)**, which powerfully combines HTML and JavaScript. Let's see how this works for displaying the variable from the previous section:

src/App.jsx

```
const title = 'React';

function App() {
  return (
    <div>
      <h1>Hello {title}</h1>
    </div>
  );
}

export default App;
```

Either start your application again with npm run dev (or check whether your application still runs) and look for the displayed (read: rendered) title in the browser. The output should read "Hello React". If you change the variable in the source code, the browser should reflect that change.

Changing the variable in the source code and seeing the change reflected in the browser is not solely connected to React, but also to the underlying development server when we start our application on the command line. Any time one of our files changes, the development server notices it and reloads all affected files for the browser. The bridge between React and the development server which makes this behavior possible is called **React Fast Refresh** (prior to that it was **React Hot Loader**) on React's side and **Hot Module Replacement** on the development server's side.

Next, try to define a HTML input field (read: <input> tag) and a HTML label (read: <label> tag) in your JSX yourself. It should also be possible to focus the input field when clicking the label either by nesting the input field in the label or by using dedicated HTML attributes for both. The following code snippet will show you the book's implementation of this task and you may be surprised that HTML slightly differs when used in JSX:

src/App.jsx

```
const title = 'React';

function App() {
  return (
    <div>
      <h1>Hello {title}</h1>

      <label htmlFor="search">Search: </label>
      <input id="search" type="text" />
    </div>
  );
}

export default App;
```

For our input field and label combination, we specified three HTML attributes: htmlFor, id, and type. The type attribute is kinda mandatory and has nothing to do with focusing the input field when clicking the label. However, while id and type should be familiar from native HTML, htmlFor might be new to you.

The htmlFor reflects the for attribute in vanilla HTML. You may be wondering why this attribute differs from native HTML. JSX replaces a handful of internal HTML attributes caused by internal implementation details of React itself. However, you can find all the supported HTML attributes[30] in React's documentation. Since JSX is closer to JavaScript than to HTML, React uses the camelCase[31] naming convention. Expect to come across more JSX-specific attributes like className and onClick instead of class and onclick, as you learn more about React.

When using HTML in JSX, React internally translates all HTML attributes to JavaScript where certain words such as class or for are reserved during the rendering process. Therefore React came up with replacements such as className and htmlFor for them. However, once the actual HTML is rendered for the browser, the attributes get translated back to their native variant.

---

[30]https://bit.ly/2Z42zcK
[31]https://bit.ly/3jljQFn

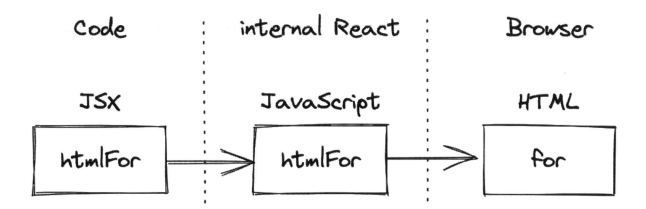

We will revisit the HTML input field and its label for further implementation details with JavaScript later. For now, in order to contrast how HTML and JavaScript are used in JSX, let's use more complex JavaScript data types in JSX. Instead of defining a JavaScript string primitive like title, define a JavaScript object called welcome which has a title (e.g. 'React') and a greeting (e.g. 'Hey') as properties. Afterward, try to render both properties of the object in JSX side by side in the <h1> tag.

The following code snippet will show you the solution to the task. Before we have defined a JavaScript string primitive to be displayed in the App component. Now, the same can be done with a JavaScript object by accessing its properties within JSX:

src/App.jsx

```
const welcome = {
  greeting: 'Hey',
  title: 'React',
};

function App() {
  return (
    <div>
      <h1>
        {welcome.greeting} {welcome.title}
      </h1>

      <label htmlFor="search">Search: </label>
      <input id="search" type="text" />
    </div>
  );
}

export default App;
```

While HTML can be used almost (except for the attributes) in its native way in JSX, everything in curly braces can be used to interpolate JavaScript in it. For example, you could define a function that returns the title and execute it within the curly braces:

src/App.jsx

```
function getTitle(title) {
  return title;
}

function App() {
  return (
    <div>
      <h1>Hello {getTitle('React')}</h1>

      <label htmlFor="search">Search: </label>
      <input id="search" type="text" />
    </div>
  );
}

export default App;
```

JSX is a syntax extension to JavaScript. In the past, JavaScript files which made use of JSX had to use[32] the *.jsx* instead of the *.js* extension. However, these days several build tools (read: compiler/bundler) can be configured to acknowledge JSX in a .js file[33]. If they are configured this way, they will transpile JSX to JavaScript. Tools like Vite embrace the *.jsx* extension though, because it makes it more explicit for developers.

Code Playground

```
const title = 'React';

// JSX ...
const myElement = <h1>Hello {title}</h1>;

// ... gets transpiled to JavaScript
const myElement = React.createElement('h1', null, `Hello ${title}`);

// ... gets rendered as HTML by React
<h1>Hello React</h1>
```

---

[32]https://bit.ly/3tT0DDD
[33]https://www.robinwieruch.de/minimal-react-webpack-babel-setup/

JSX enables developers to express what should be rendered by mixing up HTML with JavaScript. Whereas the previous way of thinking was to decouple markup (read: HTML) from logic (read: JavaScript), React puts all of it together as one unit in a React component. As you can see from the last code snippet, React does not require you to use JSX at all, instead it's possible to use methods like `createElement()`. However, most people find it more intuitive to use JSX for its declarative nature instead of using JavaScript methods (here: methods offered by React) which only allow one to express the UI imperatively.

Initially invented for React, JSX gained popularity in other modern libraries and frameworks as well. These days, it's not strictly coupled to React, but people are usually connecting it to React. Anyway, JSX is one of my favorite things when being asked about React[34]. Without any extra templating syntax (except for the curly braces), we are able to use JavaScript in HTML. Every JavaScript data structure, from primitive to complex, can be used within HTML with the help of JSX.

Exercises:

- Compare your source code against the author's source code[35].
  - Recap all the source code changes from this section[36].
  - Optional: If you are using TypeScript, check out the author's source code here[37].
- Beginner: Read more about JavaScript Variables[38].
  - Beginner: Define more primitive and complex JavaScript data types and render them in JSX.
  - Advanced: Try to render a JavaScript array in JSX by using the array's built-in `map()` method to return JSX for each item in the list. If it's too complicated, don't worry, because you will learn more about this in the next section.
- Optional: Leave feedback for this section[39].

Interview Questions:

- Question: What is JSX in React?
  - Answer: JSX is a syntax extension for JavaScript recommended by React for describing what the UI should look like.
- Question: Can JSX be directly rendered by browsers?
  - Answer: No, browsers can't understand JSX. It needs to be transpiled to regular JavaScript using tools like Babel.
- Question: Is JSX mandatory in React?
  - Answer: No, JSX is not mandatory, but it's a widely used and convenient way to write React components.
- Question: How do you render a variable in JSX?
  - Answer: Use curly braces `{}` to embed variables in JSX, like `{myVariable}`.

---

[34]https://bit.ly/3aZbdM0
[35]https://bit.ly/3S51Lfu
[36]https://bit.ly/3vLjctL
[37]https://bit.ly/3SukC3A
[38]https://www.robinwieruch.de/javascript-variable/
[39]https://forms.gle/R6y6kEqGPACLrXmP8

Lists in React

When working with data in JavaScript, most often the data comes as an array of objects. Therefore, we will learn how to render a list of items in React next. In order to prepare you for rendering lists in React, let's recap one of the most common data manipulation methods: the array's built-in map() method[40]. It is used to iterate over each item of a list in order to return a new version of each item:

Code Playground

```
const numbers = [1, 2, 3, 4];

const exponentialNumbers = numbers.map(function (number) {
  return number * number;
});

console.log(exponentialNumbers);
// [1, 4, 9, 16]
```

In React, the array's built-in map() method is used to transform a list of items into JSX by returning JSX for each item. In the following, we want to display a list of items (here: JavaScript objects) in React. First, we will define the array outside of the component. Afterward, try yourself to render each object with its title property in React by inlining the array's map() method in JSX:

src/App.jsx

```
const list = [
  {
    title: 'React',
    url: 'https://reactjs.org/',
    author: 'Jordan Walke',
    num_comments: 3,
    points: 4,
    objectID: 0,
  },
  {
    title: 'Redux',
    url: 'https://redux.js.org/',
    author: 'Dan Abramov, Andrew Clark',
    num_comments: 2,
    points: 5,
    objectID: 1,
  },
];
```

[40]https://mzl.la/3B3a7tf

```
function App() { ... }

// note the ... as placeholder
// which is use for source code that didn't change
// and isn't relevant for this code snippet

export default App;
```

Each item in the list has a title, an url, an author, an identifier (objectID), points – which indicate the popularity of an item – and a count of comments (num_comments). The property names are chosen this way, because they resemble real world data that we are going to use later. They don't fit the desired naming conventions[41] for JavaScript though, because one of them uses an underscore for example.

Next, we'll render the list inlined in JSX with the array's built-in map() method. Hence we won't map from one JavaScript data type to another, but instead return JSX that renders each item of the list:

src/App.jsx

```
function App() {
  return (
    <div>
      <h1>My Hacker Stories</h1>

      <label htmlFor="search">Search: </label>
      <input id="search" type="text" />

      <hr />

      <ul>
        {list.map(function (item) {
          return <li>{item.title}</li>;
        })}
      </ul>
    </div>
  );
}
```

Actually, rendering a list of items in React was one of my personal JSX "Aha"-moments. Without any made up templating syntax, it's possible to use JavaScript to map from an array of JavaScript

---

[41]https://www.robinwieruch.de/javascript-naming-conventions/

objects to a list of HTML elements. That's what JSX is for the developer in the end: just JS mixed with HTML.

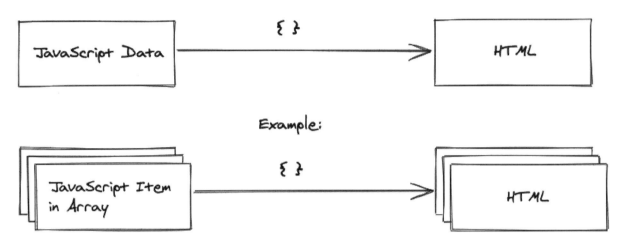

Finally React displays each item now. But there is one important piece missing. If you check your browser's developer tools, you should see a warning showing up in the "Console"-tab which says that every React element in a list should have a key assigned to it. The key is an HTML attribute and should be a stable identifier. Fortunately, our items come with such a stable identifier, because they have an id (here: objectId):

src/App.jsx

```
function App() {
  return (
    <div>
      ...

      <ul>
        {list.map(function (item) {
          return <li key={item.objectID}>{item.title}</li>;
        })}
      </ul>
    </div>
  );
}
```

The key attribute is used for one specific reason: Whenever React has to re-render a list, it checks whether an item has changed. When using keys, React can efficiently exchange the changed items. When not using keys, React may update the list inefficiently. Take the following example where a new item gets appended at the start of the list.

The key is not difficult to find, because usually when having data in the shape of an array, we can use each item's stable identifier (e.g. `id` property). However, sometimes you do not have an `id`, so you need to come up with another identifier (e.g. `title` if it does not change and if it's unique in the array). As last resort, you can use the index of the item in the list too:

Code Playground

```
<ul>
  {list.map(function (item, index) {
    return (
      <li key={index}>
        {/* only use an index as last resort */}
        {/* and by the way: that's how you do comments in JSX */}

        {item.title}
      </li>
    );
  })}
</ul>
```

Usually using an index should be avoided though, because it comes with the same rendering performance issues from above. In addition, it can cause actual bugs in the UI[42] whenever the order of items changes (e.g. re-ordering, appending or removing items). However, as last resort, if the list does not change its order in any way, using the index is fine.

So far, we are only displaying the `title` of each item. Go ahead and render the item's `url`, `author`, `num_comments`, and `points` as well. In the special case of the `url`, use an HTML anchor HTML element (read: `<a>` tag) that surrounds the `title`. Try it yourself! For guidance, the following solution will show you how the book implements this to be prepared for the next sections:

---

[42]https://www.robinwieruch.de/react-list-key/

src/App.jsx

```
function App() {
  return (
    <div>

      ...

      <ul>
        {list.map(function (item) {
          return (
            <li key={item.objectID}>
              <span>
                <a href={item.url}>{item.title}</a>
              </span>
              <span>{item.author}</span>
              <span>{item.num_comments}</span>
              <span>{item.points}</span>
            </li>
          );
        })}
      </ul>
    </div>
  );
}
```

The array's `map()` method is inlined concisely in your JSX for rendering a list. Within the `map()` method, we have access to each object and its properties. The `url` property of each item is used as `href` attribute for the anchor HTML element. Not only can JavaScript in JSX be used to display elements, but also to assign HTML attributes dynamically. This section only scratches the surface of how powerful it is to mix JavaScript and HTML, however, using an array's `map()` method and assigning HTML attributes should give you a good first impression.

Exercises:

- Compare your source code against the author's source code[43].
  - Recap all the source code changes from this section[44].
  - Optional: If you are using TypeScript, check out the author's source code here[45].
- Recap the standard built-in array methods[46], especially *map*, *filter*, and *reduce*, which are available in JavaScript.

---

[43]https://bit.ly/48YGefo
[44]https://bit.ly/3O1N0ZK
[45]https://bit.ly/484qh6p
[46]https://mzl.la/3b9V9rf

- Extend the list with some more items to make the example more realistic.
- Practice using different JavaScript expressions in JSX.
- Optional: Leave feedback for this section[47].

Interview Questions:

- Question: How to render a list of items in JSX?
  - Answer: Use map() to iterate over the array and return JSX elements for each item.
- Question: What happens if you return `null` instead of the JSX?
  - Answer: Returning `null` in JSX is allowed. It's always used if you want to render nothing.
- Question: What does the term "JSX expressions" refer to?
  - Answer: JSX expressions are JavaScript expressions embedded within curly braces in JSX, allowing dynamic content.
- Question: Can you embed HTML directly within JSX?
  - Answer: Yes, you can embed HTML directly within JSX, but it's generally discouraged due to security risks. Use dangerouslySetInnerHTML cautiously.
- Question: How do you comment in JSX?
  - Answer: Use curly braces for JavaScript comments, like {/* Your comment here */}.

---

[47]https://forms.gle/aZmLFjEdSMTk9Thk9

Meet another React Component

Components are the foundation of every React application. With a growing React project, you will get more and more components to manage. Each component encapsulates functionalities (e.g. rendering a list of items). So far we've only been using the App component. This will not end up well, because components should scale with your application's size. So instead of making one component larger and more complex over time, we'll split one component into multiple components eventually. Therefore, we'll start with a new List component which extracts functionalities from the App component:

src/App.jsx

```
const list = [ ... ];

function App() { ... }

function List() {
  return (
    <ul>
      {list.map(function (item) {
        return (
          <li key={item.objectID}>
            <span>
              <a href={item.url}>{item.title}</a>
            </span>
            <span>{item.author}</span>
            <span>{item.num_comments}</span>
            <span>{item.points}</span>
          </li>
        );
      })}
    </ul>
  );
}
```

Then the new List component can be used in the App component where we have been using the inlined HTML elements previously:

src/App.jsx

```
function App() {
  return (
    <div>
      <h1>My Hacker Stories</h1>

      <label htmlFor="search">Search: </label>
      <input id="search" type="text" />

      <hr />

      <List />
    </div>
  );
}
```

You've just created your first React component. With this example in mind, we can see how components encapsulate meaningful tasks while contributing to the greater good of a larger React project. Extracting a component is a task that you will perform very often as a React developer, because it's always the case that a component will grow in size and complexity. Go ahead and extract the label and input elements from the App component into their own Search component. The following code snippet shows how the book would solve this task:

src/App.jsx

```
function App() {
  return (
    <div>
      <h1>My Hacker Stories</h1>

      <Search />

      <hr />

      <List />
    </div>
  );
}

function Search() {
  return (
    <div>
      <label htmlFor="search">Search: </label>
```

```
        <input id="search" type="text" />
    </div>
  );
}
```

Finally, we have three components in our application: App, List, and Search. Generally speaking, a React application consists of many hierarchical components; which we can put into the following categories. The following illustration assumes that we have split out an Item component from the List component as well – which helps us to clarify the taxonomy.

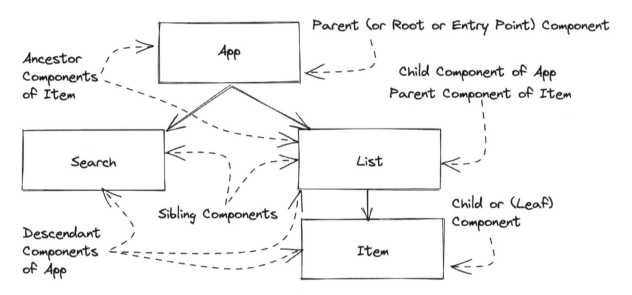

React applications have **component hierarchies** (also called **component trees**). There is usually one uppermost **entry point component** (e.g. App) that spans a tree of components below it. The App is the **parent component** of the List and Search, so the List and Search are **child components** of the App component and **sibling components** to each other. The illustration takes it one step further where the Item component is a child component of the List. In a component tree, there is always a **root component** (e.g. App), and the components that don't render any other components are called **leaf components** (e.g. List/Search component in our current source code or Item/Search component from the illustration). All components can have zero, one, or many child components.

You can see how a React application grows in size by creating more components which are connected in one hierarchy. Usually you will start out with the App component from where you grow your component tree. Either you know the components you wanna create beforehand or you start with one component and extract components from it eventually. For a beginner, it may be difficult to know when to create a new component or when to extract a component from another component. Usually it happens naturally whenever a component gets too big in size/complexity or whenever you see natural boundaries in domains/functionality (e.g. List component renders a list of items, Search component renders a search form). In the end, each component represents a single unit in your application which makes the application maintainable and predictable.

Exercises:

- Compare your source code against the author's source code[48].
  - Recap all the source code changes from this section[49].
  - Optional: If you are using TypeScript, check out the author's source code here[50].
- We can't extract an Item component from the List component (like in the illustration) yet, because we don't know how to pass individual items from the list to each Item component. Think about a way to do it.
- Optional: Leave feedback for this section[51].

Interview Questions:

- Question: Why is it beneficial to extract components in React?
  - Answer: Extracting components promotes reusability, maintainability, and a cleaner component structure.
- Question: How do you decide when to extract a component?
  - Answer: Extract a component when you find repeated UI patterns or functionality within your code.
- Question: What is the process of extracting a component called in React?
  - Answer: It's called refactoring, specifically extracting a component to improve code organization.
- Question: Is it possible to extract components across different files?
  - Answer: Yes, extracting components into separate files promotes better file organization and modularity.

---

[48]https://bit.ly/3S5rDb5
[49]https://bit.ly/47Ed7MY
[50]https://bit.ly/3SuMogq
[51]https://forms.gle/EZENmy48zvDP82NL7

React Component Instantiation

You have learned how to *declare* a component (e.g. function List() { ... }) and how to *instantiate* (e.g. ‹List /›) it. In this section, we will intensify this learning by going through an analogy and the terminology. We will start with the analogy by using the JavaScript class. Technically, JavaScript classes and React components are not related, which is important to note, but it is still a fitting analogy for you to understand the concept of a component by using something you may have used in the past.

A class is most often used in object-oriented programming languages. JavaScript as a multi-paradigm programming language allows functional programming and object-oriented programming to co-exist side-by-side. To recap JavaScript classes for object-oriented programming, consider the following *Person* class:

Code Playground

```
class Person {
  constructor(firstName, lastName) {
    this.firstName = firstName;
    this.lastName = lastName;
  }

  getName() {
    return this.firstName + ' ' + this.lastName;
  }
}
```

Each class has a constructor that takes arguments and assigns them to the class instance when instantiating it. A class can also define functions that are associated with the instance (e.g. getName()) which are called **methods** or **class methods**. Now, declaring the Person class once is just one part; instantiating it is the other. The class declaration is the blueprint of its capabilities and usage occurs when an instance is created with the new statement. If a JavaScript class declaration exists, one can create *multiple* instances of it:

Code Playground

```
// class declaration
class Person { ... }

// class instantiation
const robin = new Person('Robin', 'Wieruch');

console.log(robin.getName());
// "Robin Wieruch"
```

```
// another class instantiation
const dennis = new Person('Dennis', 'Wieruch');

console.log(dennis.getName());
// "Dennis Wieruch"
```

The concept of a JavaScript class with declaration and instantiation is similar to a React component, which also has only *one* component declaration, but can have *multiple* component instances:

src/App.jsx

```
// declaration of App component
function App() {
  return (
    <div>
      ...

      {/* creating an instance of List component */}
      <List />
      {/* creating another instance of List component */}
      <List />
    </div>
  );
}

// declaration of List component
function List() { ... }
```

Once we've defined a **component**, we can use it as an **element** anywhere in our JSX. The element produces an **instance** of your component, or in other words, the component gets instantiated. You can create as many instances of a component as you want as long as you have a component declaration. It's not much different from a JavaScript class declaration and instantiation, however, as mentioned before, technically a JavaScript class and React component are not the same. Just their usage makes it convenient to demonstrate their similarities.

Exercises:

- Read more about component, element, and instance in React[52].
  - Familiarize yourself with the terms *component declaration*, *component instance*, and *element.*

---

[52]https://www.robinwieruch.de/react-element-component/

- Experiment by creating multiple component instances of a List component.
- If we keep treating the `list` variable as a global variable, every List component would use the same `list`. Think about how it could be possible to give each List component its own `list` variable.
- Optional: Leave feedback for this section[53].

---

[53]https://forms.gle/sf1UMNR58v3NsRUSA

React DOM

We have learned about component declaration/instantiation and have already seen it in action for the List and Search components. However, at the very beginning we started with the declaration of the App component yet never came across its instantiation. It must be there, otherwise the App component and all of its descendant components in the component hierarchy would not render.

Open the *src/main.jsx* file to the see App components instantiation with the ‹App /› element. The file may differ a bit from your file, however, the following snippet shows all the essential aspects of it:

src/main.jsx

```
import React from 'react';
import ReactDOM from 'react-dom/client';
import App from './App.jsx';
import './index.css';

ReactDOM.createRoot(document.getElementById('root')).render(
  <React.StrictMode>
    <App />
  </React.StrictMode>
);
```

There are two libraries imported at the beginning of the file: react and react-dom. While React is used for the day to day business of a React developer, React DOM is usually used once in a React application to hook React into the native HTML world. Open the *index.html* file on the side and spot the HTML element where the id attribute equals "root". That's exactly the element where React inserts itself into the HTML to bootstrap the entire React application – starting with the App component.

In the JavaScript file, the createRoot() method expects the HTML element that is used to instantiate React. There we are using JavaScript's built-in getElementById() method to return the HTML element that we have seen in the *index.html* file. Once we have the root object, we can call render() on the returned root object with JSX as parameter which usually represents the entry point component (also called root component). Normally the entry point component is the instance of the App component, but it can be any other JSX too:

Code Playground

```
const title = 'React';

ReactDOM.createRoot(document.getElementById('root')).render(
  <h1>Hello {title}</h1>
);
```

Essentially React DOM is everything that's needed to integrate React into any website which uses HTML. If you start a React application from scratch, there is usually only one ReactDOM.createRoot() call in your application. However, if you happen to work on a legacy application that used something else than React before, you may see multiple ReactDOM.createRoot() calls, because only certain areas of the application are powered by React.

Anyway, do you recall the introduction about the rise of single-page applications that are powered by only a small HTML file and a large JavaScript file? You can see how everything fits together now. While one small HTML file (here: *index.html*) and one large JavaScript file (here: compiled and bundled *src/main.jsx* and *src/App.jsx* files) are transferred from web server to browser, the JavaScript file(s) are mostly responsible to render all the HTML in the browser. The HTML file is only there to request the JavaScript file and to render the HTML element where React inserts itself. From there, React calls all of its needed function components to render itself as component hierarchy.

Exercises:

- Read more about React's createRoot[54].
- Read more about React's StrictMode[55].
- Optional: Leave feedback for this section[56].

---

[54]https://bit.ly/3vx3uT2
[55]https://bit.ly/48TUA0k
[56]https://forms.gle/zSqHUhmsuQ35vqoj9

React Component Declaration

We have declared multiple React components so far. Since these components are so called function components, we can leverage the different ways of declaring functions in JavaScript for them. So far, we have used the standard function declaration, though arrow functions can be used more concisely and therefore can establish a new standard for declaring function components:

Code Playground

```
// function declaration
function App() { ... }

// arrow function expression
const App = () => { ... }
```

Equipped with this knowledge, go through your React project and refactor all function declarations to arrow function expressions. While this refactoring can be applied to function components, it can also be used for any other functions that are used in the project. We will go ahead as well and refactor all the function component's function declarations to arrow function expressions:

src/App.jsx

```
const App = () => {
  return ( ... );
};

const Search = () => {
  return ( ... );
};

const List = () => {
  return ( ... );
};
```

As said, not only function components can be refactored, but also other functions like the callback function[57] that we have used for the array's map() method:

---

[57]https://www.robinwieruch.de/javascript-callback-function/

src/App.jsx

```
const List = () => {
  return (
    <ul>
      {list.map((item) => {
        return (
          <li key={item.objectID}>
            ...
          </li>
        );
      })}
    </ul>
  );
};
```

Moreover, if an arrow function's only purpose is to return a value and it doesn't have any business logic in between, you can remove the **block body** (curly braces) of the function. In a **concise body**, an **implicit return statement** is attached, so you can remove the return statement. Check out the following demonstration:

Code Playground

```
// with block body
const addOne = (count) => {
  // perform any task in between

  return count + 1;
};

// with concise body as multi line
const addOne = (count) =>
  count + 1;

// with concise body as one line
const addOne = (count) => count + 1;
```

Let's see this in action for the Search component:

src/App.jsx

```
const Search = () => (
  <div>
    <label htmlFor="search">Search: </label>
    <input id="search" type="text" />
  </div>
);
```

This can be done for the App and List components as well, because they only return JSX and don't perform any task in between. In addition, it also applies to the arrow function that's used in the map() method:

src/App.jsx

```
const App = () => (
  <div>
    . . .
  </div>
);

const List = () => (
  <ul>
    {list.map((item) => (
      <li key={item.objectID}>
        . . .
      </li>
    ))}
  </ul>
);
```

All JSX is more concise now, because it omits the function statement, the curly braces, and the return statement. However, it's important to remember this is an optional step and that it's acceptable to use function declarations over arrow function expressions and block bodies with curly braces over concise bodies with implicit returns for arrow functions.

Often block bodies will be necessary to introduce more business logic between function signature and return statement. Be sure to understand this refactoring concept, because we'll move quickly from arrow function components with and without block bodies as we go. Which one we use will depend on the requirements of the component:

Code Playground

```
const App = () => {
  // perform a task in between

  return (
    <div>
      ...
    </div>
  );
};
```

As a rule of thumb, use either function declarations or arrow function expressions for your component declarations throughout your application. Both versions are fine to use, but make sure that you and your team working on the project share the same implementation style. In addition, while an implicit return statement when using an arrow function expressions makes your component declaration more concise, you may introduce tedious refactorings from concise to block body when you need to perform tasks between function signature and the return statement. So you may want to keep your arrow function expression with a block body (like in the last code snippet) all the time.

Exercises:

- Compare your source code against the author's source code[58].
  - Recap all the source code changes from this section[59].
  - Optional: If you are using TypeScript, check out the author's source code here[60].
- Familiarize yourself with arrow functions with block body and explicit return and concise body without return (implicit return).
- Optional: Read more about JavaScript arrow functions[61].
- Optional: Leave feedback for this section[62].

Interview Questions:

- Question: How do you declare a function component using a function declaration?
  - Answer: Use the function keyword, like `function MyComponent() {...}`.
- Question: How do you declare a function component using an arrow function expression?
  - Answer: Use the arrow function syntax, like `const MyComponent = () => {...};`.

---

[58]https://bit.ly/3U2fu9g
[59]https://bit.ly/3O7JLzI
[60]https://bit.ly/3SJbE42
[61]https://mzl.la/3BYCOcp
[62]https://forms.gle/iWSchmqasbZUWUpT8

Handler Function in JSX

We have learned a lot about React components, but there are no interactions yet. If you happen to develop an application with React, there will come a time where you have to implement a user interaction. The best place to get started in our project is the Search component – which already comes with an input field element.

In native HTML, we can add event handlers[63] on elements by using the addEventListener() method programmatically on a DOM node. In React, we are going to discover how to add handlers in JSX the declarative way. First, refactor the Search component's function from a concise body to a block body, so that we can add implementation details prior the return statement:

src/App.jsx

```
const Search = () => {
  // perform a task in between

  return (
    <div>
      <label htmlFor="search">Search: </label>
      <input id="search" type="text" />
    </div>
  );
};
```

Next, define a function, which can be either a function declaration or arrow function expression, for the change event of the input field. In React, this function is called an **(event) handler**. Afterward, the function can be passed to the onChange attribute (JSX named attribute) of the HTML input field:

src/App.jsx

```
const Search = () => {
  const handleChange = (event) => {
    // synthetic event
    console.log(event);
    // value of target (here: input HTML element)
    console.log(event.target.value);
  };

  return (
    <div>
      <label htmlFor="search">Search: </label>
      <input id="search" type="text" onChange={handleChange} />
```

---
[63]https://mzl.la/2ZbTcYZ

```
      </div>
    );
};
```

After opening your application in a web browser, open the browser's developer tools "Console"-tab to see the logging occur after you type into the input field. What you see is called a **synthetic event** as a JavaScript object and the input field's internal value.

React's synthetic event is essentially a wrapper around the browser's native event[64]. Since React started as a library for single-page applications, there was the need for enhanced functionalities on the event to prevent the native browser behavior[65]. For example, in native HTML submitting a form triggers a page refresh. However, in React this page refresh should be prevented, because the developer should take care about what happens next. Anyway, if you happen to need access to the native HTML event, you could do so by using `event.nativeEvent`, but after several years of React development I never ran into this case myself.

After all, this is how we pass HTML elements in JSX handler functions to add listeners for user interactions. Always pass functions to these handlers, not the return value of the function, except when the return value is a function again. Knowing this is crucial because it's a well-known source for bugs in a React beginner's application:

Code Playground

```
// if handleChange is a function
// which does not return a function
// don't do this
<input onChange={handleChange()} />

// do this instead
<input onChange={handleChange} />
```

As you can see, HTML and JavaScript work well together in JSX. JavaScript in HTML can display JavaScript variables (e.g. `title` string in `<span>{title}</span>`), can pass JavaScript primitives to HTML attributes (e.g. `url` string to `<a href={url}>` HTML element), and can pass functions to an HTML element's attributes for handling user interactions (e.g. `handleChange` function to `<input onChange={handleChange} />`). When developing React applications, mixing HTML and JavaScript in JSX will become your bread and butter.

Exercises:

- Compare your source code against the author's source code[66].

---

[64]https://mzl.la/30Dk8kt
[65]https://www.robinwieruch.de/react-preventdefault/
[66]https://bit.ly/48VWc9R

- Recap all the source code changes from this section[67].
  - Optional: If you are using TypeScript, check out the author's source code here[68].
- Read more about React's event handler[69].
  - Read more about event capturing and bubbling in React[70].
- In addition to the onChange attribute, add a onBlur attribute with an event handler to your input field and verify its logging in the browser's developer tools.
- Optional: Leave feedback for this section[71].

Interview Questions:

- Question: How do you define an event handler in React?
  - Answer: Create a function that handles the event, like `function handleClick() {...}`.
- Question: How do you attach an event handler in JSX?
  - Answer: Use the appropriate attribute, like `onClick={handleClick}`.
- Question: What is the common pattern for naming event handler functions?
  - Answer: Prefix the function name with "handle" followed by the event name, like `handleClick` for a click event.
- Question: Can you use arrow functions directly in the JSX for event handlers?
  - Answer: Yes, using arrow functions directly in JSX is a common pattern for concise event handlers.
- Question: How do you pass arguments to an event handler in JSX?
  - Answer: Use an arrow function to call the handler with arguments, like `onClick={() => handleClick(arg)}`.
- Question: Can you reuse event handlers across multiple elements?
  - Answer: Yes, event handlers can be reused for multiple elements with the same event type.
- Question: What is the purpose of the e.target property in an event handler?
  - Answer: It refers to the DOM element that triggered the event, allowing you to access its properties or manipulate it.
- Question: How do you access the event object in an event handler?
  - Answer: Include (event) as a parameter in the handler function, like `function handleClick(event) {...}`.
- Question: What does `event.preventDefault()` do in an event handler?
  - Answer: It prevents the default behavior of the event, such as submitting a form or following a link.
- Question: What is the purpose of the e.stopPropagation() method in an event handler?
  - Answer: It stops the event from propagating up or down the DOM tree, preventing parent or child elements from handling the same event.

---

[67] https://bit.ly/424TMUo
[68] https://bit.ly/3UrYARS
[69] https://www.robinwieruch.de/react-event-handler/
[70] https://www.robinwieruch.de/react-event-bubbling-capturing/
[71] https://forms.gle/oSKyMudmb8X1iSsv8

React Props

Currently we are using the `list` as a global variable in our project. At the beginning, we used it directly from the global scope in the App component and later in the List component. This could work if you only had one global variable and only one file with all of the components, but it isn't maintainable with multiple variables across multiple components (within multiple folders/files). By using so-called props in React, we can pass variables as information from one component to another component even though these components are not placed in the same file at some point. Let's explore how this works.

Before using props for the first time, we'll move the `list` from the global scope into the App component and give it a more self-descriptive name. Don't forget to refactor the App component's function from concise to block body in order to declare the `list` prior to the return statement:

src/App.jsx

```
const App = () => {
  const stories = [
    {
      title: 'React',
      url: 'https://reactjs.org/',
      author: 'Jordan Walke',
      num_comments: 3,
      points: 4,
      objectID: 0,
    },
    {
      title: 'Redux',
      url: 'https://redux.js.org/',
      author: 'Dan Abramov, Andrew Clark',
      num_comments: 2,
      points: 5,
      objectID: 1,
    },
  ];

  return ( ... );
};
```

Next, we'll use **React props** to pass the list of items to the List component. The variable is called `stories` in the App component and we pass it under this name to the List component. However, in the List component's instantiation, it is assigned to a new `list` HTML attribute:

src/App.jsx

```
const App = () => {
  const stories = [ ... ];

  return (
    <div>
      ...

      <List list={stories} />
    </div>
  );
};
```

Now try yourself to retrieve the list from the List component's function signature by introducing a parameter. If you find the solution yourself, congratulations for passing your first information from one component to another. If not, the following code snippet shows how it works:

src/App.jsx

```
const List = (props) => (
  <ul>
    {props.list.map((item) => (
      <li key={item.objectID}>
        ...
      </li>
    ))}
  </ul>
);
```

Everything that we pass from a parent component to a child component via the component element's HTML attribute can be accessed in the child component. The child component receives a parameter (props) as object in its function signature which includes all the passed attributes as properties (short: props).

A point to consider regarding ESLint: you might encounter an error stating, "error 'list' is missing in props validation." In an ideal scenario where React is used without TypeScript, a solution would be to incorporate prop-types[72] to provide your component with better insights into the props it receives. However, it's worth mentioning that while prop-types serve a similar purpose as TypeScript, they are considered less robust. If achieving this goal is a prerequisite for your project, it is recommended to embrace TypeScript in your React development. In cases where JavaScript is the exclusive choice, my suggestion is to disable this specific ESLint rule in your configuration file to resolve the issue.

---

[72]https://bit.ly/48Tbn3F

.eslintrc.cjs

```
rules: {
    ...
    'react/prop-types': 'off',
  },
```

Another use case for React props is the List component and its potential child component. Previously, we couldn't extract an Item component from the List component, because we didn't know how to pass each item to the extracted Item component. With this new knowledge about React props, we can perform the component extraction and pass each item along to the List component's new child component.

Before you check the following solution, try it yourself: extract an Item component from the List component and pass each item in the map() method's callback function to this new component. If you don't come up with a solution yourself after some time, check out how the book implements it:

src/App.jsx

```
const List = (props) => (
  <ul>
    {props.list.map((item) => (
      <Item key={item.objectID} item={item} />
    ))}
  </ul>
);

const Item = (props) => (
  <li>
    <span>
      <a href={props.item.url}>{props.item.title}</a>
    </span>
    <span>{props.item.author}</span>
    <span>{props.item.num_comments}</span>
    <span>{props.item.points}</span>
  </li>
);
```

Don't forget the key attribute which we introduced in an earlier section. When working with lists in JSX within a React application, it is essential to remember the significance of the key attribute. As previously discussed in a dedicated section, the key attribute plays a crucial role in the efficient rendering and updating of items within a list. By assigning a unique key to each list item, React can accurately track and manage the elements.

At the end, you should see the list rendering again. The most important fact about props: it's not allowed to change them, because they should be treated as an immutable data structure. They are only used to pass information *down* the component hierarchy. Continuing this thought, information (props) *can only* be passed from a parent to a child component and not vice versa. We will learn how to overcome this limitation later. For now, we have found our vehicle to share information from top to bottom in a React component tree.

Exercises:

- Compare your source code against the author's source code[73].
  - Recap all the source code changes from this section[74].
  - Optional: If you are using TypeScript, check out the author's source code here[75].
- Read more about how to use props in React[76].
- Optional: Leave feedback for this section[77].

Interview Questions:

- Question: What are props in React?
  - Answer: Props (short for properties) are a mechanism for passing data from a parent component to a child component.
- Question: How do you pass props to a component in JSX?
  - Answer: Include them as attributes, like `<MyComponent prop1={value1} prop2={value2} />`.
- Question: How do you access props in a function component?
  - Answer: Use the function parameters to access props, like function `MyComponent(props) {...}`.
- Question: Can you modify the value of props inside a component?
  - Answer: No, props are immutable. They should be treated as read-only.

---

[73]https://bit.ly/48XUAfE
[74]https://bit.ly/421fKaA
[75]https://bit.ly/3SzqclA
[76]https://www.robinwieruch.de/react-pass-props-to-component/
[77]https://forms.gle/APwaUSAuVAAA56sY6

React State

While it is not allowed to mutate React props as a developer, because they are only there to pass information from parent to child components, **React state** introduces a mutable data structure (read: stateful values). These stateful values get instantiated in a React component as state, can be passed with props as vehicle down to child components, but can also get mutated by using a function to modify the state. When a state gets mutated, the component with the state and all child components will re-render.

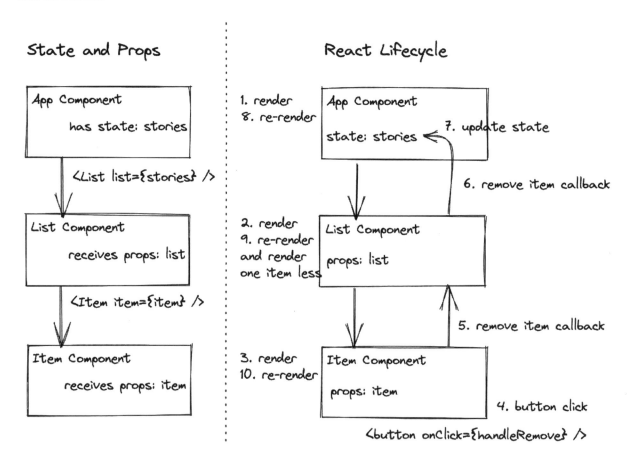

Both concepts, props and state, have cleary defined purposes: While props are used to pass information down the component hierarchy, state is used to modify information over time. Let's start with state in React with the following use case: Whenever a user types text into our HTML input field element in the Search component, the user wants to see this information (state) displayed next to it. An intuitive (but not working) approach would be the following:

src/App.jsx

```
const Search = () => {
  let searchTerm = '';

  const handleChange = (event) => {
    searchTerm = event.target.value;
  };

  return (
    <div>
      <label htmlFor="search">Search: </label>
      <input id="search" type="text" onChange={handleChange} />

      <p>
        Searching for <strong>{searchTerm}</strong>.
      </p>
    </div>
  );
};
```

When you try this in the browser, you will see that the output does not appear below the HTML input field after typing into it. However, this approach is not too far away from the actual solution. What's missing is telling React that searchTerm is a stateful value. Fortunately, React offers us a method called useState for it:

src/App.jsx

```
import * as React from 'react';

...

const Search = () => {
  const [searchTerm, setSearchTerm] = React.useState('');

  const handleChange = (event) => {
    setSearchTerm(event.target.value);
  };

  ...

};
```

By using useState, we are telling React that we want to have a stateful value which changes over time. And whenever this stateful value changes, the affected components (here: Search component) will re-render to use it (here: to display the recent value).

React's useState method takes an *initial state* as an argument – in our case it is an empty string. Furthermore, calling this method will return an array with two entries: The first entry (searchTerm) represents the *current state*. The second entry (setSearchTerm) is a function to update this state. The book will refer to this function as *state updater function*. Both entries are everything we need to display the current state (read) and to update it (write).

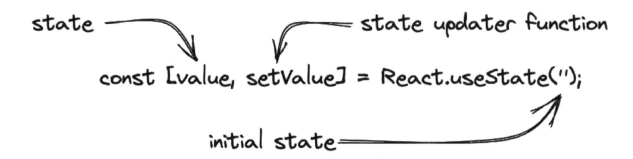

When the user types into the input field, the input field's change event uses the event handler. The handler's logic uses the event's value of the target and the state updater function to set the new state. Afterward, the component re-renders (read: the component function runs). The updated state becomes the current state (here: searchTerm) and is displayed in the component's JSX.

As an exercise, put a console.log() into each of your components. For example, the App component gets a console.log('App renders'), the List component gets a console.log('List renders') and so on. Now check your browser: For the first rendering, all loggings should appear, however, once you type into the HTML input field, only the Search component's logging should appear. React only re-renders this component (and all of its potential descendant components) after its state has changed.

Now you have heard the terms rendering and re-rendering in a technical context as well. In essence every component in a React application has one initial rendering followed by potential re-renderings. Usually the initial rendering happens when a React component gets displayed in the browser. Then whenever a side-effect occurs, like a user interaction (e.g. typing into an input field), the change is captured in React's state which forces a re-rendering of all the components affected by this change; meaning the component which manages the state and all its descendant components.

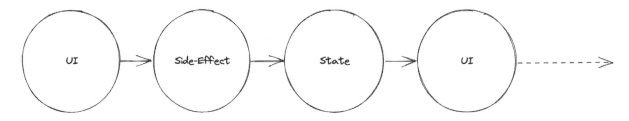

It's important to note that the useState function is called a **React hook**. It's only one of several hooks provided by React and this section only scratched the surface of hooks in React. You will learn more about them throughout the next sections. As for now, you should know that you can have as many useState hooks as you want in one or multiple components whereas state can be anything from a JavaScript string (like in this case) to a more complex data structure such as an array or object.

It is also important to note that you may see loggings twice in your browser's developer tools, a result of React's StrictMode (refer to the *src/main.jsx* file). StrictMode, functioning exclusively in the development environment, conducts extra checks and warnings to identify potential issues. When applied to the root component, it effectively highlights any problems that may arise. Later in production, there will be only one rendering.

When the UI is rendered for the first time, every rendered component's useState hook gets initialized with an initial state which gets returned as current state. Whenever the UI is re-rendered because of a state change, the useState hook uses the most recent state from its internal closure[78]. This might seem odd, as one would assume the useState gets declared from scratch every time a component's function runs. However, next to each component React allocates an object where information like state is stored in memory. Eventually the memory gets cleaned up once a component is not rendered anymore through JavaScript's garbage collection.

Exercises:

- Compare your source code against the author's source code[79].
  - Recap all the source code changes from this section[80].
  - Optional: If you are using TypeScript, check out the author's source code here[81].
- Read more about React's useState Hook[82].
- Optional: Read more about JavaScript array destructuring[83].
- Optional: Leave feedback for this section[84].

Interview Questions:

- Question: What is useState in React?
  - Answer: useState is a React hook that allows function components to manage and update state.
- Question: How do you use useState to declare state in a function component?
  - Answer: `const [state, setState] = useState(initialState);`
- Question: What triggers a re-render in React?
  - Answer: State changes or prop updates can trigger a re-render in React.
- Question: What is the purpose of the initial state in useState?
  - Answer: It sets the initial value of the state variable and only applies during the first render.

---

[78]https://www.robinwieruch.de/javascript-closure/
[79]https://bit.ly/3U3B799
[80]https://bit.ly/3vw4M0z
[81]https://bit.ly/4bn9DSm
[82]https://www.robinwieruch.de/react-usestate-hook/
[83]https://mzl.la/3ncC7WI
[84]https://forms.gle/ZJNbQqq3Lw3RiD4H9

- Question: How do you update state using useState?
  - Answer: Use the second entry returned by useState to update the state.
- Question: Does calling setState trigger an immediate re-render?
  - Answer: No, React batches state updates and performs re-renders asynchronously for performance reasons.
- Question: What is the difference between using multiple useState calls and a single useState call with an object?
  - Answer: Using multiple calls creates independent state variables, while a single call with an object allows you to manage multiple state values within one variable.
- Question: Can you directly mutate the state variable obtained from useState?
  - Answer: No, you should always use the setState function to update the state in a immutable way.
- Question: Does updating state always trigger a re-render?
  - Answer: Yes, updating state with setState triggers a re-render of the component.

Callback Handlers in JSX

While props are passed down as information from parent to child components, state can be used to change information over time. However, we don't have all the pieces yet to make our components talk to each other. When using props as vehicle to transport information, we can only talk to descendant components. When using state, we can make information stateful, but this information can also only be passed down by using props.

For example, at the moment, the Search component does not share its state with other components, so it's only used (here: displayed) and updated by the Search component. That's fine for displaying the most recent state in the Search component, however, at the end we want to use this state somewhere else. In this section for example, we want to use the state in the App component to filter the stories by searchTerm before they get passed to the List component. So we know that we could communicate to a child component via props, but do not know how to communicate the state up to a parent component (here: from Search to App component).

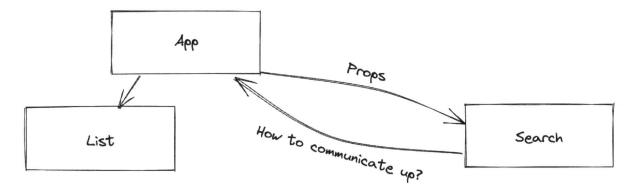

There is no way to pass information up the component tree, since props are naturally only passed downwards. However, we can introduce a **callback handler** instead: A callback handler gets introduced as event handler (A), is passed as function in props to another component (B), is executed there as handler (C), and *calls back* to the place it was introduced (D):

src/App.jsx

```
const App = () => {
  const stories = [ ... ];

  // A
  const handleSearch = (event) => {
    // D
    console.log(event.target.value);
  };

  return (
```

```
  <div>
    <h1>My Hacker Stories</h1>

    {/* // B */}
    <Search onSearch={handleSearch} />

    <hr />

    <List list={stories} />
  </div>
  );
};

const Search = (props) => {
  const [searchTerm, setSearchTerm] = React.useState('');

  const handleChange = (event) => {
    setSearchTerm(event.target.value);

    // C
    props.onSearch(event);
  };

  return ( ... );
};
```

Whenever a user types into the input field now, the function that is passed down from the App component to the Search component runs. This way, we can notify the App component when a user types into the input field in the Search component. Essentially a callback handler, which is just a more specific type of an event handler, becomes our implicit vehicle to communicate upwards the component tree.

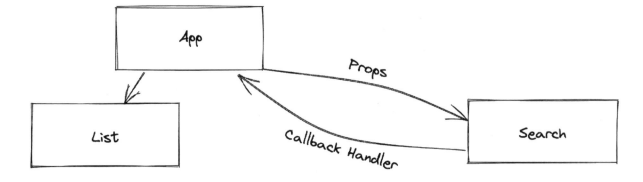

The concept of the callback handler in a nutshell: We pass a function from a parent component (App) to a child component (Search) via props; we call this function in the child component (Search), but have the actual implementation of the called function in the parent component (App). In other words, when an (event) handler is passed as props from a parent component to its child component, it becomes a callback handler. React props are always passed down the component tree and therefore functions that are passed down as callback handlers in props can be used to communicate up the component tree.

Exercises:

- Compare your source code against the author's source code[85].
  - Recap all the source code changes from this section[86].
  - Optional: If you are using TypeScript, check out the author's source code here[87].
- Revisit the concepts of (event) handler and callback handler[88] as many times as you need.
- Optional: Leave feedback for this section[89].

Interview Questions:

- Question: What is a callback handler in React?
  - Answer: A callback handler is a function passed as a prop to a child component, allowing the child to communicate with the parent.
- Question: How do you pass a callback handler to a child component?
  - Answer: Include it as a prop, like `<ChildComponent callback={handleCallback} />`.
- Question: How do you define a callback handler in a parent component?
  - Answer: Create a function in the parent component, e.g., `function handleCallback(data) {...}`.
- Question: Can a callback handler receive parameters?
  - Answer: Yes, callback handlers can receive parameters passed by the child component.
- Question: Can callback handlers be asynchronous?
  - Answer: Yes, callback handlers can be asynchronous, allowing for handling asynchronous operations.
- Question: Can you pass a callback handler through multiple layers of components?
  - Answer: Yes, you can pass callback handlers through multiple layers of components.
- Question: Can a child component have multiple callback handlers from the same parent?
  - Answer: Yes, a child component can receive and use multiple callback handlers passed from the same parent component.
- Question: Is it common to use callback handlers for form submissions in React?
  - Answer: Yes, callback handlers are commonly used for handling form submissions and updating state in parent components.

---

[85]https://bit.ly/3O6t1c8
[86]https://bit.ly/3SmJ8Fe
[87]https://bit.ly/3UnOJMQ
[88]https://www.robinwieruch.de/react-event-handler/
[89]https://forms.gle/3LoBoWKCMNT2YpnA7

Lifting State in React

In this section, we are confronted with the following task: Use the stateful searchTerm from the Search component to filter the stories by their title property in the App component before they are passed as props to the List component. So far, we have learned about how to pass information down explicitly with props and how to pass information up implicitly with callback handlers. However, if you look at the callback handler in the App component, it doesn't come natural to one on how to apply the searchTerm from the App component's handleSearch() handler as filter to the stories.

One solution could be establishing another state in the App component which captures the arriving searchTerm in the App component and then uses it for filtering the stories before they are passed to the List component as props. However, this adds duplication as a bad practice, because the searchTerm would have a state in the Search and App components then. So think about it another way: If the App component is interested in the searchTerm state to filter the stories, why not instantiate the state in the App component instead of in the Search component in the first place?

We will move the useState hook from the Search component to the App component, use the state updater function in the provided callback handler, and use the callback handler in the Search component to pass the event to the parent component. Then, whenever a user types into the input field, the state in the App component will update. Afterward, we will use the new state in the App component to filter() the stories before they are passed to the List component. The following implementation demonstrates the first part of it:

src/App.jsx

```
const App = () => {
  const stories = [ ... ];

  const [searchTerm, setSearchTerm] = React.useState('');

  const handleSearch = (event) => {
    setSearchTerm(event.target.value);
  };

  return (
    <div>
      <h1>My Hacker Stories</h1>

      <Search onSearch={handleSearch} />

      <hr />

      <List list={stories} />
    </div>
```

```
  );
};

const Search = (props) => (
  <div>
    <label htmlFor="search">Search: </label>
    <input id="search" type="text" onChange={props.onSearch} />
  </div>
);
```

We learned about the callback handler previously, because it helps us to keep an open communication channel from child component (here: Search component) to parent component (here: App component). Now, the Search component doesn't manage the state anymore, but only passes up the event to the App component via a callback handler after the text is entered into the HTML input field. From there, the App component updates its state. The process of moving state from one component to another, like we did in the last code snippet, is called **lifting state**. Next, you could still display the searchTerm again in the App component (from state, when using searchTerm) or Search component (from props, when passing the searchTerm state down as props).

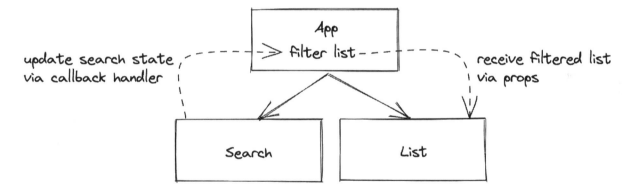

Rule of thumb: Always manage state at a component level where every component that's interested in it is one that either manages the state (using information directly from state, e.g. App component) or a component below the state managing component (using information from props, e.g. List or Search components). If a component below needs to update the state (e.g. Search), pass a callback handler down to it which allows this particular component to update the state above in the parent component. If a component below needs to use the state (e.g. displaying it), pass it down as props.

Finally, by managing the search state in the App component, we can filter the stories with the stateful searchTerm before passing them as list prop to the List component. Try it yourself by using the array's built-in filter() method in combination with the stories and the searchTerm before consulting the following implementation:

src/App.jsx

```
const App = () => {
  const stories = [ ... ];

  const [searchTerm, setSearchTerm] = React.useState('');

  const handleSearch = (event) => {
    setSearchTerm(event.target.value);
  };

  const searchedStories = stories.filter(function (story) {
    return story.title.includes(searchTerm);
  });

  return (
    <div>
      <h1>My Hacker Stories</h1>

      <Search onSearch={handleSearch} />

      <hr />

      <List list={searchedStories} />
    </div>
  );
};
```

Here, the JavaScript array's built-in filter method[90] is used to create a new filtered array. The filter() method takes a function as an argument, which accesses each item in the array and returns true or false. If the function returns true, meaning the condition is met, the item stays in the newly created array; if the function returns false, it's removed:

---

[90]https://mzl.la/3BYFAOR

Code Playground

```
const words = [
  'spray',
  'limit',
  'elite',
  'exuberant',
  'destruction',
  'present'
];

const filteredWords = words.filter(function (word) {
  return word.length > 6;
});

console.log(filteredWords);
// ["exuberant", "destruction", "present"]
```

The `filter()` method could be made more concise by using an arrow function with an immediate return:

src/App.jsx

```
const App = () => {
  ...

  const searchedStories = stories.filter((story) =>
    story.title.includes(searchTerm)
  );

  ...
};
```

That's all to the refactoring steps of the inlined function for the `filter()` method. There are many variations to it – and it's not always simple to keep a good balance between readability and conciseness – however, I feel like keeping it concise whenever possible keeps it most of the time readable as well.

What's not working very well yet: The `filter()` method checks whether the `searchTerm` is present as string in the `title` property of each story, but it's case sensitive. If we search for "react", there is no filtered "React" story in your rendered list. Try to fix this problem yourself by making the `filter()` method's condition case insensitive with the pure force of JavaScript. The following code snippet shows you how to achieve it by lower casing the `searchTerm` and the `title` of the story:

src/App.jsx

```
const App = () => {
  ...

  const searchedStories = stories.filter((story) =>
    story.title.toLowerCase().includes(searchTerm.toLowerCase())
  );

  ...
};
```

Now you should be able to search for "eact", "React", or "react" and see one of two displayed stories. Congratulations, you have just added your first real interactive feature to your application by leveraging state – to derive a filtered list of stories – and props – by passing a callback handler to the Search component.

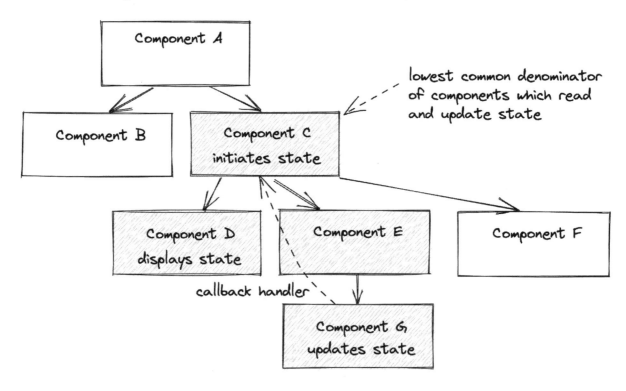

After all, knowing where to instantiate state in React turns out to be an important skill in every React developer's career. The state should always be there where all components which depend on the state can read (via props) and update (via callback handler) it. These are all descendant components of the component which instantiates the state.

Exercises:

- Compare your source code against the author's source code[91].
  - Recap all the source code changes from this section[92].
  - Optional: If you are using TypeScript, check out the author's source code here[93].
- Read more about lifting state in React[94].
- Optional: Leave feedback for this section[95].

Interview Questions:

- Question: What is lifting state in React?
  - Answer: Lifting state refers to the practice of moving the state from a child component to its parent component.
- Question: Why would you lift state in React?
  - Answer: To share and manage state at a higher level, making it accessible to multiple child components.
- Question: How do you lift state in React?
  - Answer: Move the state and related functions to a common ancestor (usually a parent) component.
- Question: Can multiple child components share the same lifted state?
  - Answer: Yes, lifting state allows multiple child components to share the same state.
- Question: What's the advantage of lifting state over using local state in a component?
  - Answer: Lifting state promotes sharing state among components.
- Question: What is the role of callbacks in lifting state?
  - Answer: Callback functions are used to pass data from child to parent components when lifting state.
- Question: Can a child component modify the state of a parent component directly through a callback handler?
  - Answer: No, the child component can invoke the callback to notify the parent, and the parent can decide how to update its state.
- Question: Is it necessary to lift all state to the top-level parent component?
  - Answer: No, only lift state to a level where it needs to be shared among multiple components.
- Question: How does lifting state contribute to better component reusability?
  - Answer: Lifting state allows stateful logic to be concentrated in a common ancestor, making components more reusable.

---

[91]https://bit.ly/48U6Rlq
[92]https://bit.ly/3U3Fhhh
[93]https://bit.ly/49k1Cf9
[94]https://www.robinwieruch.de/react-lift-state/
[95]https://forms.gle/EqJGjxCM1Xzw9S6g7

React Controlled Components

HTML elements come with their internal state which is not coupled to React. Confirm this thesis yourself by checking how your HTML input field is implemented in your Search component. While we provide essential attributes like id and type in addition to a handler (here: onChange), we do not tell the element its value. However, it does show the correct value when a user types into it.

Now try the following: When initializing the searchTerm state in the App component, use 'React' as initial state instead of an empty string. Afterward, open the application in the browser. Can you spot the problem? Spend some time on your own figuring out what happens here and how to fix this problem.

While the stories have been filtered respectively to the new initial searchTerm in the last section, the HTML input field doesn't show the value in the browser. Only when we start typing into the input field do we see the changes reflected in it. That's because the input field doesn't know anything about React's state (here: searchTerm), it only uses its handler to communicate (see handleSearch()) its internal state to React state. And once a user starts typing into the input field, the HTML element keeps track of these changes itself. However, if we want to get things right, the HTML should know about the React state. Therefore, we need to provide the current state as value to it:

src/App.jsx

```
const App = () => {
  const stories = [ ... ];

  const [searchTerm, setSearchTerm] = React.useState('React');

  ...

  return (
    <div>
      <h1>My Hacker Stories</h1>

      <Search search={searchTerm} onSearch={handleSearch} />

      ...
    </div>
  );
};

const Search = (props) => (
  <div>
    <label htmlFor="search">Search: </label>
    <input
```

```
      id="search"
      type="text"
      value={props.search}
      onChange={props.onSearch}
    />
  </div>
);
```

Now both states are synchronized. Instead of giving the HTML element the freedom of keeping track of its internal state, it uses React's state by leveraging the element's value attribute instead. Whenever the HTML element emits a change event, the new value is written to React's state and re-renders the components. Then the HTML element uses the recent state as value again.

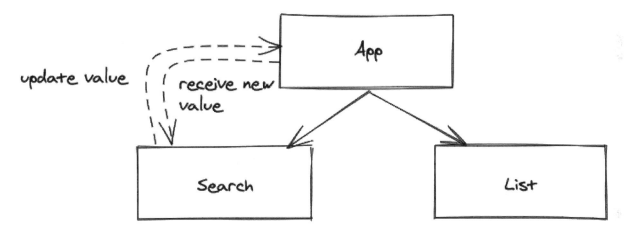

Earlier the HTML element did its own thing, but now we are in control of it by feeding React's state into it. Now, while the input field became explicitly a **controlled element**, the Search component became implicitly a **controlled component**. As a React beginner, using controlled components is important, because you want to enforce a predictable behavior. Later though, there may be cases for uncontrolled components too.

Exercises:

- Compare your source code against the author's source code[96].
  - Recap all the source code changes from this section[97].
  - Optional: If you are using TypeScript, check out the author's source code here[98].
- Read more about controlled components in React[99].
- Optional: Leave feedback for this section[100].

---

[96]https://bit.ly/3U9zc3f
[97]https://bit.ly/4b09Omb
[98]https://bit.ly/3w3A5Ah
[99]https://www.robinwieruch.de/react-controlled-components/
[100]https://forms.gle/7VYTww2EQiPkFnaR8

Interview Questions:

- Question: What is a controlled component in React?
  - Answer: A controlled component is a component whose form elements are controlled by React state.
- Question: How do you create a controlled input in React?
  - Answer: Set the input value attribute to a state variable and provide an onChange handler to update the state.
- Question: What is the role of the value prop in a controlled input element?
  - Answer: The value prop sets the current value of the input, making it a controlled component.
- Question: How do you handle a controlled checkbox in React?
  - Answer: Use the checked attribute and provide an onChange handler to update the corresponding state.
- Question: How do you clear the value of a controlled component?
  - Answer: Set the state variable to an empty or null value to clear the value of a controlled component.
- Question: What are the potential downsides of using controlled components?
  - Answer: Controlled components can lead to verbose code, especially in forms with many input elements.

Props Handling (Advanced)

Props are passed from parent to child down the component tree. Since we use props to transport information from component to component frequently, and sometimes via other components which are in between, it is useful to know a few tricks to make passing props more convenient.

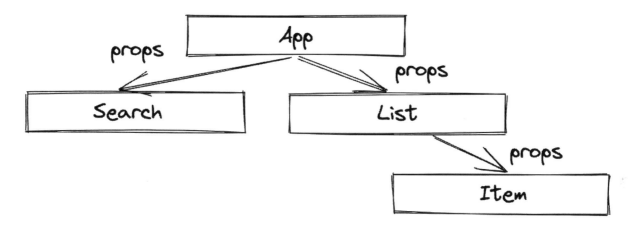

The following refactorings are recommended for you to learn different JavaScript/React patterns, though you can still build complete React applications without them. Consider these as advanced props techniques that will make your React code for certain scenarios more concise, readable, and maintainable.

Props Destructuring via Object Destructuring

React props are just a JavaScript object, otherwise we couldn't access props.list or props.onSearch in our React components. Since props is an object which just passes information from one component to another component, we can apply a couple JavaScript tricks to it. For example, accessing an object's properties with modern JavaScript object destructuring[101]:

Code Playground

```
const user = {
  firstName: 'Robin',
  lastName: 'Wieruch',
};

// without object destructuring
const firstName = user.firstName;
const lastName = user.lastName;
```

---

[101]https://mzl.la/30KbXTC

```
// with object destructuring
const { firstName, lastName } = user;
```

When we need to access various properties of an object, employing a single line of code rather than multiple lines is often a more straightforward and elegant approach. This is why object destructuring is commonly utilized in JavaScript. Before delving into the upcoming code snippet, attempt to apply this understanding to the React props within our Search component.

Now, let's explore how we can employ props destructuring. Initially, we need to refactor the Search component's arrow function from a concise body to a block body. Subsequently, we can implement the destructuring of the props object within the function body:

src/App.jsx

```
const Search = (props) => {
  const { search, onSearch } = props;

  return (
    <div>
      <label htmlFor="search">Search: </label>
      <input
        id="search"
        type="text"
        value={search}
        onChange={onSearch}
      />
    </div>
  );
};
```

That's a basic destructuring of the props object in a React component, so that the object's properties can be used conveniently in the component. However, we also had to refactor the Search component's arrow function from concise body into block body to access the properties of props with the object destructuring in the component function's body. This would happen quite often if we followed this pattern and it wouldn't make things easier for us, because we would constantly have to refactor our components. We can take all this one step further by destructuring the props object right away in the function signature of our component, omitting the function's block body of the component again:

src/App.jsx

```jsx
const Search = ({ search, onSearch }) => (
  <div>
    <label htmlFor="search">Search: </label>
    <input
      id="search"
      type="text"
      value={search}
      onChange={onSearch}
    />
  </div>
);
```

React's props are rarely used in components by themselves; rather, all the information that is contained in the props object is used. By destructuring the props object right away in the component's function signature, we can conveniently access all information without dealing with its props container. The List and Item components can perform the same props destructuring:

src/App.jsx

```jsx
const List = ({ list }) => (
  <ul>
    {list.map((item) => (
      <Item key={item.objectID} item={item} />
    ))}
  </ul>
);

const Item = ({ item }) => (
  <li>
    <span>
      <a href={item.url}>{item.title}</a>
    </span>
    <span>{item.author}</span>
    <span>{item.num_comments}</span>
    <span>{item.points}</span>
  </li>
);
```

The use of object destructuring aligns with JavaScript's best practices and promotes a cleaner and more efficient React component structure. It allows for a more straightforward extraction of the required properties, enhancing both the clarity of the code and the overall development experience in React applications. However, we can take this one step further with some more optional advanced lessons.

Nested Destructuring

The incoming `item` parameter in the Item component has something in common with the previously discussed `props` parameter: they are both JavaScript objects. Also, even though the `item` object has already been destructured from the `props` in the Item component's function signature, it isn't directly used in the Item component. The `item` object only passes its information (object properties) to the elements.

The current solution is fine as you will see in the ongoing discussion. However, I want to show you two more variations of it, because there are many things to learn about JavaScript objects in React here. Let's get started with *nested destructuring* and how it works:

Code Playground

```
const user = {
  firstName: 'Robin',
  pet: {
    name: 'Trixi',
  },
};

// without object destructuring
const firstName = user.firstName;
const name = user.pet.name;

console.log(firstName + ' has a pet called ' + name);
// "Robin has a pet called Trixi"

// with nested object destructuring
const {
  firstName,
  pet: {
    name,
  },
} = user;

console.log(firstName + ' has a pet called ' + name);
// "Robin has a pet called Trixi"
```

The nested destructuring helps us to gather all the needed information of the `item` object in the function signature for its immediate usage in the component's elements. Even though it's not the most readable option here, note that it can still be useful in other scenarios:

src/App.jsx

```
// Variation 1: Nested Destructuring

const Item = ({
  item: {
    title,
    url,
    author,
    num_comments,
    points,
  },
}) => (
  <li>
    <span>
      <a href={url}>{title}</a>
    </span>
    <span>{author}</span>
    <span>{num_comments}</span>
    <span>{points}</span>
  </li>
);
```

In summary, nested destructuring in React proves to be a powerful and efficient technique when dealing with complex data structures, especially within nested objects or arrays in props or state. This approach simplifies the extraction of deeply nested values, making the code more concise and readable. However, nested destructuring introduces lots of clutter through indentations in the function signature. While here it's not the most readable option, it can be useful in other scenarios though.

Spread and Rest Operators

Let's take another approach with JavaScript's spread and rest operators. In order to prepare for it, we will refactor our List and Item components to the following implementation. Rather than passing the item as an object from List to Item component, we are passing every property of the item object:

src/App.jsx

```
// Variation 2: Spread and Rest Operators
// 1. Step

const List = ({ list }) => (
  <ul>
    {list.map((item) => (
      <Item
        key={item.objectID}
        title={item.title}
        url={item.url}
        author={item.author}
        num_comments={item.num_comments}
        points={item.points}
      />
    ))}
  </ul>
);

const Item = ({ title, url, author, num_comments, points }) => (
  <li>
    <span>
      <a href={url}>{title}</a>
    </span>
    <span>{author}</span>
    <span>{num_comments}</span>
    <span>{points}</span>
  </li>
);
```

Now, even though the Item component's function signature is more concise, the clutter ended up in the List component instead, because every property is passed to the Item component individually. We can improve this approach using JavaScript's spread operator[102]:

---

[102]https://mzl.la/3jetIkn

Code Playground

```
const profile = {
  firstName: 'Robin',
  lastName: 'Wieruch',
};

const address = {
  country: 'Germany',
  city: 'Berlin',
};

const user = {
  ...profile,
  gender: 'male',
  ...address,
};

console.log(user);
// {
//   firstName: "Robin",
//   lastName: "Wieruch",
//   gender: "male"
//   country: "Germany,
//   city: "Berlin",
// }
```

JavaScript's spread operator allows us to literally spread all key/value pairs of an object to another object. This can also be done in React's JSX. Instead of passing each property one at a time via props from List to Item component as before, we can use JavaScript's spread operator to pass all the object's key/value pairs as attribute/value pairs to a JSX element:

src/App.jsx

```
// Variation 2: Spread and Rest Operators
// 2. Step

const List = ({ list }) => (
  <ul>
    {list.map((item) => (
      <Item key={item.objectID} {...item} />
    ))}
  </ul>
);
```

```
const Item = ({ title, url, author, num_comments, points }) => (
  <li>
    <span>
      <a href={url}>{title}</a>
    </span>
    <span>{author}</span>
    <span>{num_comments}</span>
    <span>{points}</span>
  </li>
);
```

This refactoring made the process of passing the information from List to Item component more concise. Finally, we'll use JavaScript's rest destructuring as the icing on the cake. The JavaScript rest operation happens always as the last part of an object destructuring:

Code Playground

```
const user = {
  id: '1',
  firstName: 'Robin',
  lastName: 'Wieruch',
  country: 'Germany',
  city: 'Berlin',
};

const { id, country, city, ...userWithoutAddress } = user;

console.log(userWithoutAddress);
// {
//   firstName: "Robin",
//   lastName: "Wieruch"
// }

console.log(id);
// "1"

console.log(city);
// "Berlin"
```

Even though both have the same syntax (three dots), the rest operator shouldn't be mistaken with the spread operator. Whereas the rest operator happens on the left side of an assignment, the spread operator happens on the right side. The rest operator is always used to separate an object from some of its properties.

Now it can be used in our List component to separate the `objectID` from the item, because the `objectID` is only used as a `key` and isn't used in the Item component. Only the remaining (read: rest) item gets spread as attribute/value pairs into the Item component (as before):

src/App.jsx

```
// Variation 2: Spread and Rest Operators
// Final Step

const List = ({ list }) => (
  <ul>
    {list.map(({ objectID, ...item }) => (
      <Item key={objectID} {...item} />
    ))}
  </ul>
);

const Item = ({ title, url, author, num_comments, points }) => (
  <li>
    <span>
      <a href={url}>{title}</a>
    </span>
    <span>{author}</span>
    <span>{num_comments}</span>
    <span>{points}</span>
  </li>
);
```

In this final variation, the rest operator is used to destructure the `objectID` from the rest of the `item` object. Afterward, the `item` is spread with its key/value pairs into the Item component. While this final variation is very concise, it comes with advanced JavaScript features that may be unknown to some.

In this section, we have learned about JavaScript object destructuring which can be commonly used not only for the `props` object, but also for other objects like the `item` object which are nested within the props. We have also seen how nested destructuring can be used (Variation 1), but also how it didn't add any benefits in our case because it just made the component bigger. In the future, you are more likely to find use cases for nested destructuring which are beneficial.

Last but not least, you have learned about JavaScript's spread and rest operators, which shouldn't be confused with each other, to perform operations on JavaScript objects and to pass the `props` object from one component to another component in the most concise way. In the end, I want to point out the initial version again which we will continue to use in the next sections:

src/App.jsx

```jsx
const List = ({ list }) => (
  <ul>
    {list.map((item) => (
      <Item key={item.objectID} item={item} />
    ))}
  </ul>
);

const Item = ({ item }) => (
  <li>
    <span>
      <a href={item.url}>{item.title}</a>
    </span>
    <span>{item.author}</span>
    <span>{item.num_comments}</span>
    <span>{item.points}</span>
  </li>
);
```

It may not be the most concise, but it is the easiest to understand. Variation 1 with its nested destructuring didn't add much benefit and variation 2 added too many advanced JavaScript features (spread operator, rest operator) which are not familiar to everyone. After all, all these variations have their pros and cons. When refactoring a component, always aim for readability, especially when working in a team of people, and make sure everyone is using a common React code style.

Rules of thumb:

- Almost always use object destructuring for props in a function component's function signature, because props are rarely used themselves. Exception: When props are only passed through the component to the next child component (see when to use spread operator).
- Use the spread operator when you want to pass all key/value pairs of an object to a child component in JSX. For example, often props themselves are not used in a component but only passed along to the next component. Then it makes sense to just spread the props object {...props} to the next component.
- Use the rest operator when you only want to split out certain properties from your props object.
- Use nested destructuring only when it improves readability.

Exercises:

- Compare your source code against the author's source code[103].

---

[103]https://bit.ly/48TdhkK

   – Recap all the source code changes from this section[104].
      – Optional: If you are using TypeScript, check out the author's source code here[105].
- Read more about how to use props in React[106].
- Optional: Read more about JavaScript's destructuring assignment[107].
- Read more about JavaScript's spread operator[108] and rest operator[109].
- Get a good sense about JavaScript (e.g. destructuring, spread operator, rest destructuring) and how it relates to React (e.g. props) from the last lessons.
- Continue to use your favorite way to handle React's props. If you're still undecided, consider the variation used in the previous section.
- Optional: Leave feedback for this section[110].

Interview Questions:

- Question: How do you destructure props in a function component's parameters?
   – Answer: You can destructure props directly in the function parameters, like this: function MyComponent({ prop1, prop2 }) {...}.
- Question: Can you provide a default value while destructuring props?
   – Answer: Yes, you can provide default values during destructuring, such as { prop1 = 'default', prop2 }.
- Question: Is it necessary to destructure all props, or can you choose specific ones?
   – Answer: You can choose to destructure specific props based on your component's needs, leaving others untouched.
- Question: How is the spread operator (...) used in React props?
   – Answer: The spread operator is used to pass all properties of an object as separate props to a React component, like <MyComponent {...obj} />.
- Question: Can you use the spread operator to combine props with additional ones?
   – Answer: Yes, you can combine existing props with additional ones using the spread operator, like <MyComponent {...props} newProp={value} />.
- Question: Does the spread operator create a shallow or deep copy of an object?
   – Answer: The spread operator creates a shallow copy of an object, meaning nested objects are still references to the original.
- Question: What is the purpose of the rest operator (...rest) in React?
   – Answer: The rest operator is used to collect remaining properties into a new object, often used in combination with props destructuring.
- Question: Why is array destructuring used for React Hooks like useState and object destructuring for props?
   – Answer: A React Hook like useState returns an array whereas props are an object; hence we need to apply the appropriate operation for the underlying data structure. The benefit of having an array returned from useState is that the values can be given any name in the destructuring operation.
- Question: What is prop drilling in React?
   – Answer: Prop drilling is the process of passing props through multiple layers of components to reach a deeply nested child component.

---

[104]https://bit.ly/3SndcQQ
[105]https://bit.ly/3SL9uRm
[106]https://www.robinwieruch.de/react-pass-props-to-component/
[107]https://mzl.la/30KbXTC
[108]https://mzl.la/3jetIkn
[109]https://mzl.la/3GeJbef
[110]https://forms.gle/WNB4R6yEP1hot3tK8

React Side-Effects

A React component's returned output is defined by its props and state. Side-effects can affect this output too, because they are used to interact with third-party APIs (e.g. browser's localStorage API, remote APIs for data fetching), with HTML elements for width and height measurements, or with built-in JavaScript functions such as timers or intervals. These are only a few examples of side-effects in React components and we will get to apply one of these examples next.

At the moment, whenever you search for a term in our application you will get the result. However, once you close the browser and open it again, the search term isn't there anymore. Wouldn't it be a great user experience if our Search component could remember the most recent search, so that the application displays it in the browser whenever it restarts?

Let's implement this feature by using a side-effect to store the recent search in the browser's local storage and retrieve it upon the initial component initialization. First, use the local storage to store the searchTerm accompanied by an identifier whenever a user types into the HTML input field:

src/App.jsx

```
const App = () => {
  ...

  const handleSearch = (event) => {
    setSearchTerm(event.target.value);

    localStorage.setItem('search', event.target.value);
  };

  ...
);
```

Second, use the stored value, if a value exists, to set the initial state of the searchTerm in React's useState Hook. Otherwise, default to our initial state (here: "React") as before:

src/App.jsx

```
const App = () => {
  ...

  const [searchTerm, setSearchTerm] = React.useState(
    localStorage.getItem('search') || 'React'
  );

  ...
);
```

Good to know: JavaScript's logical OR operator[111] returns the truthy operand in this expression and is short-circuited if `localStorage.getItem('search')` returns a truthy value. It's used as a shorthand for the following implementation for setting default values:

Code Playground

```
let hasStored;
if (localStorage.getItem('search')) {
  hasStored = true;
} else {
  hasStored = false;
}

const initialState = hasStored
  ? localStorage.getItem('search')
  : 'React';
```

When using the input field and refreshing the browser tab, the browser should remember the latest search term now. Essentially we synchronized the browser's local storage with React's state: While we initialize the state with the browser's local storage's value (or a fallback), we write the new value when the handler is called to the browser's storage and the component's state.

The feature is complete, but there is one flaw that may introduce bugs in the long run: The handler function should mostly be concerned with updating the state, but it has a side-effect now. The flaw: If we use the `setSearchTerm` state updater function somewhere else in our application, we break the feature because the local storage doesn't get updated, because it is only updated in the event handler. Let's fix this by handling the side-effect at a centralized place and not in a specific handler. We'll use **React's useEffect Hook** to trigger the desired side-effect each time the `searchTerm` changes:

src/App.jsx

```
const App = () => {
  ...

  const [searchTerm, setSearchTerm] = React.useState(
    localStorage.getItem('search') || 'React'
  );

  React.useEffect(() => {
    localStorage.setItem('search', searchTerm);
  }, [searchTerm]);

  const handleSearch = (event) => {
    setSearchTerm(event.target.value);
```

---

[111]https://mzl.la/3aXxryd

```
   };


   . . .

);
```

React's useEffect Hook takes two arguments: The first argument is a function that runs our side-effect. In our case, the side-effect stores `searchTerm` into the browser's local storage. The second argument is a dependency array of variables. If one of these variables changes, the function for the side-effect is called. In our case, the function is called every time the `searchTerm` changes (e.g. when a user types into the HTML input field). In addition, it's also called initially when the component renders for the first time.

Leaving out the second argument (the dependency array) would make the function for the side-effect run on every render (initial render and update renders) of the component. If the dependency array of React's useEffect is an empty array, the function for the side-effect is only called once when the component renders for the first time. After all, the hook lets us opt into React's component lifecycle when mounting, updating and unmounting the component. It can be triggered when the component is first mounted, but also if one of its values (state, props, derived values from state/props) is updated.

In conclusion, using React `useEffect` Hook instead of managing the side-effect in the (event) handler has made the application more robust. *Whenever* and *wherever* the `searchTerm` state is updated via `setSearchTerm`, the browser's local storage will always be in sync with it.

Exercises:

- Compare your source code against the author's source code[112].
  - Recap all the source code changes from this section[113].

  - Optional: If you are using TypeScript, check out the author's source code here[114].
- Read more about React's useEffect Hook[115].
  - Give the first argument's function a `console.log()` and experiment with React's useEffect Hook's dependency array. Check the logs for an empty dependency array too.
- Read more about using local storage with React[116].
- Try the following scenario: In your browser, backspace the search term from the input field until nothing is left there. Internally, it should be set to an empty string now. Next, refresh the browser and check what it displays. You may be wondering why it does show "React" instead of "", because "" should be the recent search. That's because JavaScript's logical OR evaluates "" to false and thus takes "React" as the true value. If you want to prevent this and evaluate "" as true instead, you may want to exchange JavaScript's logical OR operator || with JavaScript's nullish coalescing operator ??[117].
  - Optional: Leave feedback for this section[118].

[112]https://bit.ly/48JDlzm
[113]https://bit.ly/3U7NwJk
[114]https://bit.ly/3HKAv0Y
[115]https://www.robinwieruch.de/react-useeffect-hook/
[116]https://www.robinwieruch.de/local-storage-react/
[117]https://mzl.la/2Z4bsU4
[118]https://forms.gle/iCtVZHYt2XRNfAcBA

Interview Questions:

- Question: What is useEffect in React?
  - Answer: useEffect is a hook in React that allows function components to perform side effects.
- Question: Can you use multiple useEffect hooks in one component?
  - Answer: Yes, you can use multiple useEffect hooks in a single component.
- Question: What does the second argument in useEffect represent?
  - Answer: The second argument is an array of dependencies. The effect runs when any of these dependencies change.
- Question: How do you run useEffect only once (on mount)?
  - Answer: Pass an empty dependency array ([]) as the second argument.
- Question: Can useEffect return a cleanup function?
  - Answer: Yes, the function returned from useEffect serves as a cleanup function.
- Question: What is the purpose of the cleanup function in useEffect?
  - Answer: It handles the cleanup or teardown of resources when the component unmounts or when the dependencies change.
- Question: How do you perform cleanup in useEffect for each render?
  - Answer: Return a function inside the useEffect with the cleanup logic.
- Question: Can you conditionally run useEffect based on a certain condition?
  - Answer: Yes, you can use conditional statements inside useEffect to control when it should run.
- Question: What happens if you omit the second argument in useEffect?
  - Answer: It runs the effect after every render, leading to potential performance issues.
- Question: How does useEffect contribute to avoiding race conditions in React?
  - Answer: It allows you to handle asynchronous operations and avoid race conditions by managing the order of execution.

React Custom Hooks (Advanced)

Until now, we have delved into two of React's most popular hooks: useState and useEffect. The former proves valuable for managing values that undergo changes, while the latter facilitates the inclusion of side effects in the lifecycle of React components. While there are additional hooks provided by React, our upcoming focus will be on **React custom Hooks**, involving the creation of our own hooks tailored to specific requirements.

To illustrate this concept, we will leverage our understanding of useState and useEffect to craft a new custom hook dubbed useStorageState. The primary objective of this custom hook is to ensure the synchronization of a component's state with the local storage of the browser. We will initiate our exploration by outlining how we intend to utilize this hook within our App component:

src/App.jsx

```
const App = () => {
  const stories = [ ... ];

  const [searchTerm, setSearchTerm] = useStorageState('React');

  const handleSearch = (event) => {
    setSearchTerm(event.target.value);
  };

  const searchedStories = stories.filter((story) =>
    story.title.toLowerCase().includes(searchTerm.toLowerCase())
  );

  return (
    ...
  );
};
```

With this custom hook, we can use it in a manner akin to React's native useState Hook. It provides both a state variable and a function for updating the state, taking an initial state as an argument. The underlying functionality of this hook will be designed to ensure the synchronization of the state with the local storage of the browser. If you look closely at the App component in the previous code snippet, you can see that none of the previously introduced local storage features are there anymore. Instead, we will copy and paste this functionality over to our new custom hook:

src/App.jsx

```
const useStorageState = () => {
  const [searchTerm, setSearchTerm] = React.useState(
    localStorage.getItem('search') || ''
  );

  React.useEffect(() => {
    localStorage.setItem('search', searchTerm);
  }, [searchTerm]);
};

const App = () => {
...
};
```

So far, this custom hook is just a function around the useState and useEffect hooks which we've previously used in the App component. What's missing is providing an initial state and returning the values that are needed in our App component as an array:

src/App.jsx

```
const useStorageState = (initialState) => {
  const [searchTerm, setSearchTerm] = React.useState(
    localStorage.getItem('search') || initialState
  );

  React.useEffect(() => {
    localStorage.setItem('search', searchTerm);
  }, [searchTerm]);

  return [searchTerm, setSearchTerm];
};
```

We are following two conventions of React's built-in hooks here. First, the naming convention which puts the "use" prefix in front of every hook name. And second, the returned values are returned as an array. Another goal of a custom hook should be reusability. All of this custom hook's internals are about a certain search domain, however, to make the custom hook reusable and therefore generic, we have to adjust the internal names:

src/App.jsx

```
const useStorageState = (initialState) => {
  const [value, setValue] = React.useState(
    localStorage.getItem('value') || initialState
  );

  React.useEffect(() => {
    localStorage.setItem('value', value);
  }, [value]);

  return [value, setValue];
};
```

Now we handle an abstracted "value" within the custom hook. Using it in the App component, we can name the returned current state and state updater function anything domain-related (e.g. searchTerm and setSearchTerm) with array destructuring.

There is still one problem with this custom hook. Using the custom hook more than once in a React application leads to an overwrite of the "value"-allocated item in the local storage, because it uses the same key in the local storage. To fix this, we need to pass in a flexible key. Since the key comes from outside, the custom hook assumes that it could change, so it needs to be included in the dependency array of the useEffect hook as well. Without it, the side-effect may run with an outdated key (also called *stale*) if the key changed between renders:

src/App.jsx

```
const useStorageState = (key, initialState) => {
  const [value, setValue] = React.useState(
    localStorage.getItem(key) || initialState
  );

  React.useEffect(() => {
    localStorage.setItem(key, value);
  }, [value, key]);

  return [value, setValue];
};

const App = () => {
  ...

  const [searchTerm, setSearchTerm] = useStorageState(
    'search',
    'React'
```

```
    );

    ...

};
```

With the key in place, you can use this new custom hook more than once in your application. You only need to make sure that the first argument, the key you are passing in, is a unique identifier which allocates the state in the browser's local storage under a unique key. If you happen to use the same key more than once for multiple useStorageState hook usages, then all these hooks will work on the same local storage key/value pair.

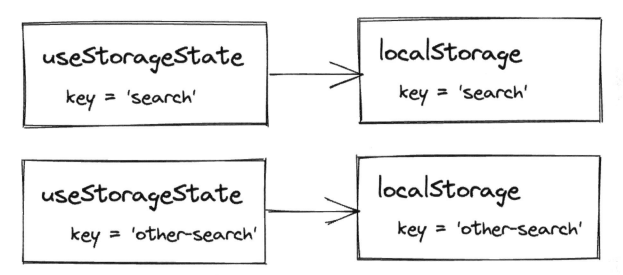

You've just created your first custom hook. If you're not comfortable with custom hooks, you can revert the changes and use the useState and useEffect hook as before in the App component. However, knowing about custom hooks gives you lots of new options. A custom hook can encapsulate non-trivial implementation details that should be kept away from a component, can be used in more than one React component, can be a composition of other hooks, and can even be open-sourced as an external library. Using your favorite search engine, you'll notice there are hundreds of React hooks that could be used in your application without worry over implementation details.

Exercises:

- Compare your source code against the author's source code[119].
  - Recap all the source code changes from this section[120].
  - Optional: If you are using TypeScript, check out the author's source code here[121].

---

[119]https://bit.ly/3vC6zkJ
[120]https://bit.ly/4aYZjjc
[121]https://bit.ly/485dY9K

- Read more about React Hooks[122] and custom React Hooks[123] to get a good understanding of them, because they are the bread and butter in React function components.
- Optional: Leave feedback for this section[124].

Interview Questions:

- Question: What are React custom hooks?
  - Answer: Custom hooks are JavaScript functions that utilize React hooks to encapsulate and reuse logic in function components.
- Question: How do you create a custom hook in React?
  - Answer: Create a function starting with "use" and use existing React hooks or other custom hooks within it.
- Question: Can custom hooks have state?
  - Answer: Yes, custom hooks can use hooks like useState.
- Question: What naming convention should custom hooks follow?
  - Answer: Custom hooks should be named with the prefix "use" to signal their association with React hooks.
- Question: Can custom hooks accept parameters?
  - Answer: Yes, custom hooks can accept parameters to make them flexible and customizable.
- Question: How do you share stateful logic between components using custom hooks?
  - Answer: Extract the shared logic into a custom hook and use it in multiple components.
- Question: Do custom hooks have access to the component's props?
  - Answer: No, custom hooks don't have direct access to the component's props. They usually accept necessary data through arguments.
- Question: Can you use multiple custom hooks in a single component?
  - Answer: Yes, you can use multiple custom hooks in a single component to leverage different pieces of reusable logic.
- Question: What's the key benefit of using custom hooks?
  - Answer: Custom hooks promote code reuse, abstraction of complex logic, and maintainability in React function components.
- Question: Can custom hooks have side effects like data fetching?
  - Answer: Yes, custom hooks can encapsulate side effects using hooks like useEffect to perform tasks such as data fetching.
- Question: Are custom hooks only for state management?
  - Answer: No, while custom hooks can manage state, they can encapsulate any reusable logic, including side effects and computations.

---

[122]https://www.robinwieruch.de/react-hooks/
[123]https://www.robinwieruch.de/react-custom-hook/
[124]https://forms.gle/5seN1Rv3ZwXmWmDR9

React Fragments

You may have noticed that all of our React components return JSX with one top-level HTML element. When we introduced the Search component a while ago, we had to add a `<div>` tag (read: container element), because otherwise the label and input elements couldn't be returned side-by-side without a wrapping top-level element:

src/App.jsx

```
const Search = ({ search, onSearch }) => (
  <div>
    <label htmlFor="search">Search: </label>
    <input
      id="search"
      type="text"
      value={search}
      onChange={onSearch}
    />
  </div>
);
```

However, there are ways to render multiple top-level elements side-by-side. A rarely used approach returns all sibling elements as an array. Since this resembles a list of elements, we would have to give each list item a mandatory `key` attribute:

src/App.jsx

```
const Search = ({ search, onSearch }) => [
  <label key="1" htmlFor="search">
    Search:{' '}
  </label>,
  <input
    key="2"
    id="search"
    type="text"
    value={search}
    onChange={onSearch}
  />,
];
```

Fortunately there exists another way of returning sibling elements side-by-side without a top-level element, because the last approach with the array doesn't turn out very readable and becomes verbose with the additional key attribute. Another solution is to use a **React fragment**:

src/App.jsx

```
const Search = ({ search, onSearch }) => (
  <React.Fragment>
    <label htmlFor="search">Search: </label>
    <input
      id="search"
      type="text"
      value={search}
      onChange={onSearch}
    />
  </React.Fragment>
);
```

A fragment wraps sibling elements into a single top-level element without adding them to the rendered output. See for yourself by inspecting the elements in your browser's development tools after using a fragment in your React component. A more popular alternative these days is using fragments in their shorthand version:

src/App.jsx

```
const Search = ({ search, onSearch }) => (
  <>
    <label htmlFor="search">Search: </label>
    <input
      id="search"
      type="text"
      value={search}
      onChange={onSearch}
    />
  </>
);
```

Both elements in the Search component - input field and label - should be still visible in your browser now. After all, whenever you don't want to introduce an intermediary element that's only there to satisfy React, you can use fragments as helper "elements".

Exercises:

- Compare your source code against the author's source code[125].
  - Recap all the source code changes from this section[126].
  - Optional: If you are using TypeScript, check out the author's source code here[127].
- Optional: Leave feedback for this section[128].

---

[125]https://bit.ly/3u4IimX
[126]https://bit.ly/3S0MLPH
[127]https://bit.ly/3HLzrtH
[128]https://forms.gle/kNpEySPZzckNe6f96

Interview Questions:

- Question: What is a Fragment in React?
  - Answer: A Fragment is a way to group multiple React elements without introducing an additional DOM element.
- Question: How do you use Fragments in JSX?
  - Answer: Wrap the elements with `<React.Fragment>` or its shorthand syntax `<>...</>`.
- Question: Why use Fragments in React?
  - Answer: Fragments allow grouping elements without adding extra nodes to the DOM, useful when a parent wrapper is not desired.
- Question: Can Fragments have keys?
  - Answer: Yes, Fragments can have keys when mapping over a list of elements.
- Question: Are Fragments required in every React component?
  - Answer: No, Fragments are optional and are typically used when a component needs to return multiple elements without a parent wrapper.
- Question: Do Fragments impact the rendered HTML structure?
  - Answer: No, Fragments do not introduce any additional nodes to the HTML structure.
- Question: Can Fragments have attributes like class or style?
  - Answer: No, Fragments themselves cannot have attributes. Attributes should be applied to the elements within the Fragment.
- Question: How does using Fragments differ from using div containers?
  - Answer: Fragments don't create an extra DOM node, providing a cleaner HTML structure compared to using div containers.

Reusable React Component

Examine the Search component more closely: Every intricate detail of its implementation is closely linked to the search feature. However, internally, the component is composed of merely a label and an input. Why should it be so tightly bound to a singular domain? This narrow association makes the component less adaptable for other functionalities within the application. Consequently, the Search component becomes impractical for tasks unrelated to searching.

Moreover, the Search component poses a risk of introducing bugs. If multiple instances of this Search component are rendered on the same page, their htmlFor/id combination is duplicated. This duplication disrupts the focus when a user clicks on one of the labels. To rectify these issues, let's enhance the Search component's reusability.

Given that the Search component lacks actual "search" functionality, making it reusable for various application features involves minimal effort. We can achieve this by introducing dynamic id and label props to the Search component, renaming the specific value and callback handler to more generic terms, and consequently, renaming the component itself:

src/App.jsx

```
const App = () => {
  ...

  return (
    <div>
      <h1>My Hacker Stories</h1>

      <InputWithLabel
        id="search"
        label="Search"
        value={searchTerm}
        onInputChange={handleSearch}
      />

      ...
    </div>
  );
};

const InputWithLabel = ({ id, label, value, onInputChange }) => (
  <>
    <label htmlFor={id}>{label}</label>
     
    <input
```

```
      id={id}
      type="text"
      value={value}
      onChange={onInputChange}
    />
  </>
);
```

While it is entirely reusable, its applicability is limited to using an input with text. To broaden its
scope and support additional input types, such as numbers (number) or phone numbers (tel), the
type attribute of the input field needs to be accessible from the outside too:

src/App.jsx

```
const InputWithLabel = ({
  id,
  label,
  value,
  type = 'text',
  onInputChange,
}) => (
  <>
    <label htmlFor={id}>{label}</label>
     
    <input
      id={id}
      type={type}
      value={value}
      onChange={onInputChange}
    />
  </>
);
```

Because we don't pass a type prop from the App component to the InputWithLabel component,
the default parameter[129] from the function signature takes over for the type. Thus, every time the
InputWithLabel component is used without a type prop, the default type will be "text".

With just a few changes we turned a specialized Search component into a more reusable InputWith-
Label component. We generalized the naming of the internal implementation details and gave the
new component a larger API surface to provide all the necessary information from the outside. We
aren't using the component elsewhere yet, but we increased its ability to handle the task if we do.

---

[129]https://mzl.la/3aUefkN

It's always a trade-off between generalization and specialization of components. In this case, we turned a highly specialized component into a generalized component. While a generalized component has a better chance of getting reused in the application, a specialized component would implement business logic for one specific use case and therefore isn't reusable at all.

Exercises:

- Compare your source code against the author's source code[130].
  - Recap all the source code changes from this section[131].
  - Optional: If you are using TypeScript, check out the author's source code here[132].
- Read more about Reusable React Components[133] and create some of these components yourself:
  - Button in React[134], Radio Button in React[135], Checkbox in React[136], Dropdown in React[137], Drag-and-Drop List in React (Advanced)[138], ...
- Before we used the text "Search:" with a ":". How would you deal with it now? Would you pass it with `label="Search:"` as prop to the InputWithLabel component or hardcode it after the `<label htmlFor={id}>{label}:</label>` usage in the InputWithLabel component? We will see how to cope with this later.
- Optional: Leave feedback for this section[139].

Interview Questions:

- Question: Why is reusability important in React?
  - Answer: Reusability promotes code efficiency, maintainability, and consistency by allowing components to be used across various parts of an application.
- Question: How can you make a React component reusable?
  - Answer: Make components more generic by using props for customizable behavior and ensuring they are not tightly coupled to specific functionalities.
- Question: How do React props contribute to reusability?
  - Answer: Props make components adaptable and reusable by allowing dynamic customization.
- Question: Can a reusable component have internal state?
  - Answer: Yes, a reusable component can have internal state by using a hook like useState.
- Question: Why is component abstraction important for reusability?
  - Answer: Abstraction hides unnecessary details, making components more versatile and easier to reuse without exposing their internal complexities.
- Question: Is it advisable to make all components in a React application reusable?
  - Answer: While reusability is beneficial, not all components need to be reusable. Often there are components which have only a single purpose and are only used once in a React application.

---

[130]https://bit.ly/3U98mIj

[131]https://bit.ly/3vDLFBP

[132]https://bit.ly/3Oun6hn

[133]https://www.robinwieruch.de/react-reusable-components/

[134]https://www.robinwieruch.de/react-button/

[135]https://www.robinwieruch.de/react-radio-button/

[136]https://www.robinwieruch.de/react-checkbox/

[137]https://www.robinwieruch.de/react-dropdown/

[138]https://www.robinwieruch.de/react-drag-and-drop/

[139]https://forms.gle/76C3LvW3kHHwdhgq5

React Component Composition

Essentially a React application is a bunch of React components arranged in the shape of a tree. When you learned about initializing components as elements in JSX, you have seen how they are used like any other HTML element in JSX. However, until now we have only used them as self-closing tags. What if there could be an opening and closing tag instead for React elements too? Entering the concept of component composition:

src/App.jsx

```
const App = () => {
  ...

  return (
    <div>
      <h1>My Hacker Stories</h1>

      <InputWithLabel
        id="search"
        value={searchTerm}
        onInputChange={handleSearch}
      >
        Search:
      </InputWithLabel>

      ...
    </div>
  );
};
```

Component composition is one of React's more powerful features. Essentially we'll discover how to use a React element in the same fashion as an HTML element by leveraging its opening and closing tag. In the previous example, instead of using the label prop from before, we inserted the text "Search:" between the component's element's tags. In the InputWithLabel component, you have access to this information via **React's children** prop now. Instead of using the label prop, use the children prop to render everything that has been rendered in between the <InputWithLabel> opening and closing tag:

src/App.jsx

```
const InputWithLabel = ({
  id,
  value,
  type = 'text',
  onInputChange,
  children,
}) => (
  <>
    <label htmlFor={id}>{children}</label>
     
    <input
      id={id}
      type={type}
      value={value}
      onChange={onInputChange}
    />
  </>
);
```

Now the React component's elements behave similarly to native HTML. Everything that's passed between a component's elements can be accessed as `children` in the component and be rendered. Sometimes when using a React component, you want to have more freedom from the outside regarding what to render on the inside of a component:

src/App.jsx

```
const App = () => {
  ...

  return (
    <div>
      <h1>My Hacker Stories</h1>

      <InputWithLabel
        id="search"
        value={searchTerm}
        onInputChange={handleSearch}
      >
        <strong>Search:</strong>
      </InputWithLabel>

      ...
```

```
      </div>
   );
};
```

With the React children prop, we can compose React components into each other. We've used it with a string and with a string wrapped in an HTML `<strong>` element, but it doesn't end here. You can pass React elements via React children as well – which you should definitely explore more as an exercise.

Exercises:

- Compare your source code against the author's source code[140].
  - Recap all the source code changes from this section[141].
  - Optional: If you are using TypeScript, check out the author's source code here[142].
- Read more about Component Composition in React[143].
- Optional: Leave feedback for this section[144].

Interview Questions:

- Question: What does "children" refer to in React components?
  - Answer: "Children" in React refers to the content placed between the opening and closing tags of a component.
- Question: How can you access and render the "children" of a React component?
  - Answer: Use the `props.children` property to access and render the content placed within a component.
- Question: Can a React component have multiple children?
  - Answer: Yes, but would use attributes instead, like `<MyComponent slotOne={<em>1</em>}` `slotTwo={<em>2</em>} />` which can then be accessed via `props.slotOne` and `props.slotTwo` in the component.
- Question: Can you pass React components as "children" to another component?
  - Answer: Yes, React components can be passed as "children" to other components, allowing for composability.
- Question: What is the purpose of the React.Children utility in React?
  - Answer: The React.Children utility provides methods for working with and manipulating the "children" of a React component.
- Question: How do you iterate over and manipulate each child in a React component?
  - Answer: Use React.Children.map or React.Children.forEach to iterate over and perform operations on each child of a component.
- Question: Can you have a component without any "children" in React?
  - Answer: Yes, a component can exist without any "children" by not placing content between its opening and closing tags.
- Question: What is the difference between "children" and other props in React?
  - Answer: "Children" refers specifically to the content between tags, while other props are key-value pairs passed to a component.

---

[140]https://bit.ly/492oks5

[141]https://bit.ly/3u4KkDB

[142]https://bit.ly/3uvSg0S

[143]https://www.robinwieruch.de/react-component-composition/

[144]https://forms.gle/L2GgfHVjAAwbqudq8

Imperative React

Imperative programming involves providing explicit step-by-step instructions, detailing how a program should perform a task. In contrast, declarative programming focuses on specifying the desired outcome without specifying every procedural step. Declarative code is often considered more concise, readable, and maintainable.

React uses a declarative programming approach. Instead of manually manipulating the Document Object Model (DOM) for UI updates, developers declare the desired UI state, and React manages the rendering process. This declarative approach enhances code readability and scalability, abstracting away the complexities of DOM manipulation and enabling the creation of dynamic user interfaces with a higher level of abstraction.

When you implement JSX, you tell React what elements you want to see, not how to create these elements. When you implement a hook for state, you tell React what you want to manage as a stateful value and not how to manage it. And when you implement an event handler, you do not have to assign a listener imperatively:

Code Playground

```
// imperative JavaScript + DOM API
element.addEventListener('click', () => {
  // do something
});

// declarative React
const App = () => {
  const handleClick = () => {
    // do something
  };

  return (
    <button
      type="button"
      onClick={handleClick}
    >
      Click
    </button>
  );
};
```

However, there are cases when we will not want everything to be declarative. For example, sometimes you want to have imperative access to rendered elements, most often as a side-effect, in cases such as these:

- read/write access to elements via the DOM API:
  - reading (here: measuring) an element's width or height
  - writing (here: setting) an input field's focus state
- implementation of more complex animations:
  - setting transitions
  - orchestrating transitions
- integration of third-party libraries:
  - D3[145] is a popular imperative chart library

Due to the verbosity and counterintuitive nature of imperative programming in React, we will only explore a brief example illustrating how to imperatively set the focus of an input field. Conversely, for the declarative approach, you can achieve the same outcome by setting the autoFocus attribute of the input field:

src/App.jsx

```
const InputWithLabel = ({ ... }) => (
  <>
    <label htmlFor={id}>{children}</label>
     
    <input
      id={id}
      type={type}
      value={value}
      autoFocus
      onChange={onInputChange}
    />
  </>
);


// note that `autoFocus` is a shorthand for `autoFocus={true}`
// every attribute that is set to `true` can use this shorthand
```

This works, but only if one of the reusable components is rendered. For example, if the App component renders two InputWithLabel components, only the last rendered component receives the autoFocus flag on its render. However, since we have a reusable React component here, we can pass a dedicated prop which lets the developer decide whether the input field should have an active autoFocus:

---

[145]https://d3js.org

src/App.jsx

```
const App = () => {
  ...

  return (
    <div>
      <h1>My Hacker Stories</h1>

      <InputWithLabel
        id="search"
        value={searchTerm}
        isFocused
        onInputChange={handleSearch}
      >
        <strong>Search:</strong>
      </InputWithLabel>

      ...
    </div>
  );
};
```

Again, using just `isFocused` as an attribute is equivalent to `isFocused={true}`. Within the component, use the new prop for the input field's `autoFocus` attribute:

src/App.jsx

```
const InputWithLabel = ({
  id,
  value,
  type = 'text',
  onInputChange,
  isFocused,
  children,
}) => (
  <>
    <label htmlFor={id}>{children}</label>
     
    <input
      id={id}
      type={type}
      value={value}
      autoFocus={isFocused}
```

```
      onChange={onInputChange}
    />
  </>
);
```

The feature works, yet it's a declarative implementation. We are telling React *what* to do and not *how* to do it. Even though it's possible to do it with the declarative approach (which is the recommended way), let's refactor this scenario to an imperative approach. We want to execute the focus() method programmatically on the input field's element via the DOM API once it has been rendered:

src/App.jsx

```
const InputWithLabel = ({
  id,
  value,
  type = 'text',
  onInputChange,
  isFocused,
  children,
}) => {
  // A
  const inputRef = React.useRef();

  // C
  React.useEffect(() => {
    if (isFocused && inputRef.current) {
      // D
      inputRef.current.focus();
    }
  }, [isFocused]);

  return (
    <>
      <label htmlFor={id}>{children}</label>
       
      {/* B */}
      <input
        ref={inputRef}
        id={id}
        type={type}
        value={value}
        onChange={onInputChange}
      />
    </>
```

```
  );
};
```

All the essential steps are marked with comments that are explained step by step:

- (A) First, create a `ref` with **React's useRef Hook**. This `ref` object is a persistent value which stays intact over the lifetime of a React component. It comes with a property called `current`, which, in contrast to the `ref` object, can be changed.
- (B) Second, the `ref` is passed to the element's JSX-reserved `ref` attribute and thus element instance gets assigned to the changeable `current` property.
- (C) Third, opt into React's lifecycle with React's useEffect Hook, performing the focus on the element when the component renders (or its dependencies change).
- (D) And fourth, since the `ref` is passed to the element's `ref` attribute, its `current` property gives access to the element. Execute its focus programmatically as a side-effect, but only if `isFocused` is set and the `current` property is existent.

Essentially that's the whole example of how to move from declarative to imperative programming in React. In this case, it's possible to use either the declarative or imperative approach as you experienced first hand. However, it's not always possible to use the declarative approach, so the imperative approach can be performed whenever it's necessary. Since we didn't cover `ref` and `useRef` in much detail here, because it is a more rarely used feature in React, I suggest reading the additional article from the exercises for a more in-depth understanding.

Exercises:

- Compare your source code against the author's source code[146].
    - Recap all the source code changes from this section[147].
    - Optional: If you are using TypeScript, check out the author's source code here[148].
- Read more about refs in React[149] and optionally check out the following tutorials which are using refs:
    - Create an image from a React component with a ref[150]
    - Create a Slider component with a ref[151]
    - Create a custom hook with a ref[152]
- Read more about why frameworks matter[153].
- Optional: Leave feedback for this section[154].

[146]https://bit.ly/3U5XDP4
[147]https://bit.ly/48Pl9DY
[148]https://bit.ly/494zUDw
[149]https://www.robinwieruch.de/react-ref/
[150]https://www.robinwieruch.de/react-component-to-image/
[151]https://www.robinwieruch.de/react-slider/
[152]https://www.robinwieruch.de/react-custom-hook-check-if-overflow/
[153]https://www.robinwieruch.de/why-frameworks-matter/
[154]https://forms.gle/nABoW2tKAPd1yVkv7

Interview Questions:

- Question: What is useRef in React?
    - Answer: useRef is a hook in React that provides a mutable object called a ref, which can hold a mutable value and persists across renders.
- Question: How is useRef different from useState in React?
    - Answer: Unlike useState, useRef doesn't trigger a re-render when its value changes. It's often used for mutable values that don't affect the rendering.
- Question: Can useRef be used to hold a mutable value that persists across renders?
    - Answer: Yes, the primary purpose of useRef is to hold mutable values that persist across renders without causing re-renders.
- Question: What is the common use case for useRef in React?
    - Answer: A common use case is accessing and interacting with the DOM, as useRef can hold a reference to a DOM element.
- Question: Can useRef be used to trigger re-renders in React?
    - Answer: No, changing the value of a ref created with useRef does not trigger a re-render.
- Question: Can useRef be used to persist values between function calls?
    - Answer: Yes, useRef values persist across renders, making them suitable for persisting values between function calls without triggering re-renders.
- Question: How can you access the current value of a ref created with useRef?
    - Answer: Use myRef.current to access the current value of a ref created with useRef.

Inline Handler in JSX

In this section, you'll learn about inline handlers as a new fundamental building block in React. Simultaneously, we'll implement our next feature that enables the removal of items from the list. Before delving further, feel free to attempt this task independently, as it can be solved without prior knowledge of inline handlers. Provided below are step-by-step instructions. If you encounter difficulties, proceed to read this section for the solution. If you successfully find a solution on your own, compare it with the book's solution, which utilizes inline handlers.

Task: The application renders a list of items and allows its users to filter the list via a search feature. Next the application should render a button next to each list item which allows its users to remove the item from the list.

Optional Hints:

- The list of items needs to become a stateful value (here: stateful array) with useState in order to manipulate it (e.g. removing an item) later.
- Every list item renders a button with a click handler. When clicking the button, the item gets removed from the list by manipulating the state.
- Since the stateful list resides in the App component, one needs to use callback handlers to enable the Item component to communicate up to the App component for removing an item by its identifier.

Now we want to check out how to implement this feature step by step. At the moment, the list of items (here: stories) that we have in our App component is an unstateful variable. We can filter the rendered list with the search feature, but the list itself stays intact. The filtered list is just a derived state through a third-party (here: searchTerm), but we do not manipulate the actual list yet. To gain control over the list, make it stateful by using it as initial state in React's useState Hook. The returned values from the array are the current state (stories) and the state updater function (setStories):

src/App.jsx

```
const initialStories = [
  {
    title: 'React',
    url: 'https://reactjs.org/',
    author: 'Jordan Walke',
    num_comments: 3,
    points: 4,
    objectID: 0,
  },
  {
    title: 'Redux',
    url: 'https://redux.js.org/',
```

```
      author: 'Dan Abramov, Andrew Clark',
      num_comments: 2,
      points: 5,
      objectID: 1,
    },
  ];


  ...


  const App = () => {
    const [searchTerm, setSearchTerm] = ...

    const [stories, setStories] = React.useState(initialStories);


    ...
  };
```

The application behaves the same because the stories, now returned as a stateful list from React's useState Hook, are still filtered into searchedStories and displayed in the List component. Just the origin where the stories are coming from has changed. But we are not modifying the stories yet. Next, we will write an event handler which removes an item from the list:

src/App.jsx

```
const App = () => {
  ...

  const [stories, setStories] = React.useState(initialStories);

  const handleRemoveStory = (item) => {
    const newStories = stories.filter(
      (story) => item.objectID !== story.objectID
    );

    setStories(newStories);
  };


  ...


  return (
    <div>
      <h1>My Hacker Stories</h1>


        ...
```

```
      <hr />

      <List list={searchedStories} onRemoveItem={handleRemoveStory} />
    </div>
  );
};
```

The callback handler in the App component – which will be used in the List/Item components eventually – receives the item as an argument which should be removed from the list. Based on this information, the function filters the current stories by removing all items that don't meet its condition. The returned stories – where the desired item (story) has been removed – are then set as a new state and passed to the List component. Since a new state is set, the App component and all components below (e.g. List/Item components) will render again and thus display the new state of stories.

However, what's missing is how the List/Item components are using this new functionality which modifies the state in the App component. The List component itself does not use this new callback handler, but only passes it on to the Item component:

src/App.jsx

```
const List = ({ list, onRemoveItem }) => (
  <ul>
    {list.map((item) => (
      <Item
        key={item.objectID}
        item={item}
        onRemoveItem={onRemoveItem}
      />
    ))}
  </ul>
);
```

Finally, the Item component uses the incoming callback handler as a function in a new handler. In this handler, we will pass the specific item to it. Moreover, an additional button element is needed to trigger the actual event:

src/App.jsx

```
const Item = ({ item, onRemoveItem }) => {
  const handleRemoveItem = () => {
    onRemoveItem(item);
  };

  return (
    <li>
      <span>
        <a href={item.url}>{item.title}</a>
      </span>
      <span>{item.author}</span>
      <span>{item.num_comments}</span>
      <span>{item.points}</span>
      <span>
        <button type="button" onClick={handleRemoveItem}>
          Dismiss
        </button>
      </span>
    </li>
  );
};
```

So far in this section, we have made the list of stories stateful with React's useState Hook, passed the still searched stories down as props to the List component, and implemented a callback handler (handleRemoveStory) and handler (handleRemoveItem) to be used in their respective components to remove a story by clicking on a button. In order to implement this feature, we applied many lessons learned from before: state, props, handlers, and callback handlers. The feature works and you may have arrived at the same or a similar solution yourself.

Let's enter the topic of inline handlers: You may have noticed that we had to introduce an additional handleRemoveItem handler in the Item component which is in charge of executing the incoming onRemoveItem callback handler. We had to introduce this extra event handler to pick up the item as argument for the callback handler.

If you want to make this more elegant though, you can use an **inline handler** which allows you to execute the callback handler function in the Item component right in the JSX. There are two solutions using the incoming onRemoveItem function in the Item component as an inline handler. First, using JavaScript's bind method:

src/App.jsx

```
const Item = ({ item, onRemoveItem }) => (
  <li>
    <span>
      <a href={item.url}>{item.title}</a>
    </span>
    <span>{item.author}</span>
    <span>{item.num_comments}</span>
    <span>{item.points}</span>
    <span>
      <button type="button" onClick={onRemoveItem.bind(null, item)}>
        Dismiss
      </button>
    </span>
  </li>
);
```

Using JavaScript's bind method[155] on a function allows us to bind arguments directly to that function that should be used when executing it. The bind method returns a new function with the bound argument attached. In contrast, the second and more popular solution is to use an inline arrow function, which allows us to sneak in arguments like the item:

src/App.jsx

```
const Item = ({ item, onRemoveItem }) => (
  <li>
    <span>
      <a href={item.url}>{item.title}</a>
    </span>
    <span>{item.author}</span>
    <span>{item.num_comments}</span>
    <span>{item.points}</span>
    <span>
      <button type="button" onClick={() => onRemoveItem(item)}>
        Dismiss
      </button>
    </span>
  </li>
);
```

While using an inline handler is more concise than using a normal event handler, it can also be more difficult to debug because JavaScript logic may be hidden in JSX. It becomes even more verbose if

---

[155]https://mzl.la/3ncEkBu

the inline arrow function encapsulates more than one line of implementation logic by using a block body instead of a concise body:

Code Playground

```
const Item = ({ item, onRemoveItem }) => (
  <li>
    ...
    <span>
      <button
        type="button"
        onClick={() => {
          // do something else

          // note: avoid using complex logic in JSX

          onRemoveItem(item);
        }}
      >
        Dismiss
      </button>
    </span>
  </li>
);
```

As a rule of thumb: It's okay to use inline handlers if they do not obscure critical implementation details. If inline handlers need to use a block body, because there are more than one line of code executed, it's about time to extract them as normal event handlers. After all, in this case all handler versions are readable and therefore acceptable.

Exercises:

- Compare your source code against the author's source code[156].
  - Recap all the source code changes from this section[157].
  - Optional: If you are using TypeScript, check out the author's source code here[158].
- Read more about how to add[159], update[160], remove[161] items in a list.
- Read more about computed properties in React[162].
- Review handlers, callback handlers, and inline handlers[163].
- Optional: Leave feedback for this section[164].

[156]https://bit.ly/4b4LQX2
[157]https://bit.ly/3u85gcS
[158]https://bit.ly/3UwzjWz
[159]https://www.robinwieruch.de/react-add-item-to-list
[160]https://www.robinwieruch.de/react-update-item-in-list/
[161]https://www.robinwieruch.de/react-remove-item-from-list
[162]https://www.robinwieruch.de/react-computed-properties/
[163]https://www.robinwieruch.de/react-event-handler/
[164]https://forms.gle/19NvNYMk2RUKTDyZ6

Interview Questions:

- Question: What is an inline function in React?
  - Answer: An inline function in React is often used as a function defined directly within the JSX.
- Question: What is the advantage of using inline functions for event handlers in React?
  - Answer: Inline functions allow you to pass additional parameters easily.
- Question: What is the alternative to using inline functions for event handlers in React?
  - Answer: Creating handler functions outside the render method and passing references to them can be an alternative.
- Question: What is the syntax for creating an inline function in a React JSX event handler?
  - Answer: Use arrow function syntax directly within the event handler attribute, like `onClick={() => myFunction()}`.

React Asynchronous Data

We have two interactions in our application: searching the list and removing items from the list. While the first interaction is a fluctuant modification through a third-party state (searchTerm) applied on the list, the second interaction is a non-reversible deletion of an item from the list. However, the list we are dealing with is still just sample data. What about preparing our application to deal with real data instead?

Usually, data from a remote backend/database arrives asynchronously for client-side applications like React. Thus it's often the case that we must render a component before we can initiate the data fetching. In the following, we will start by simulating this kind of asynchronous data with our sample data in the application. Later, we will replace the sample data with real data fetched from a real remote API. We start off with a function that returns a promise with data in its shorthand version once it resolves. The resolved object holds the previous list of stories:

src/App.jsx

```
const initialStories = [ ... ];

const getAsyncStories = () =>
  Promise.resolve({ data: { stories: initialStories } });
```

In the App component, instead of using the initialStories, use an empty array for the initial state. We want to start off with an empty list of stories and simulate fetching these stories asynchronously. In a new useEffect hook, call the function and resolve the returned promise as a side-effect. Due to the empty dependency array, the side-effect only runs once the component renders for the first time:

src/App.jsx

```
const App = () => {

  ...

  const [stories, setStories] = React.useState([]);

  React.useEffect(() => {
    getAsyncStories().then(result => {
      setStories(result.data.stories);
    });
  }, []);

  ...

};
```

Even though the data should arrive asynchronously when we start the application, it appears to arrive synchronously, because it's rendered immediately. Let's change this by giving it a bit of a realistic delay, because every network request to a remote API would come with a delay. First, remove the shorthand version for the promise:

src/App.jsx

```
const getAsyncStories = () =>
  new Promise((resolve) =>
    resolve({ data: { stories: initialStories } })
  );
```

And second, when resolving the promise, delay it for 2 seconds:

src/App.jsx

```
const getAsyncStories = () =>
  new Promise((resolve) =>
    setTimeout(
      () => resolve({ data: { stories: initialStories } }),
      2000
    )
  );
```

Once you start the application again, you should see a delayed rendering of the list. The initial state for the stories is an empty array and therefore nothing gets rendered in the List component. After the App component is rendered, the side-effect hook runs once to fetch the asynchronous data. After resolving the promise and setting the data in the component's state, the component renders again and displays the list of asynchronously loaded stories.

This section was only the first stepping stone to asynchronous data in React. Instead of having the data there from the beginning, we resolved the data asynchronously from a promise. However, we only moved our stories from being synchronous to asynchronous data. It's still sample data though and we will learn how to fetch real data eventually.

Exercises:

- Compare your source code against the author's source code[165].
  - Recap all the source code changes from this section[166].
  - Optional: If you are using TypeScript, check out the author's source code here[167].
- Optional: Read more about JavaScript Promises[168].

---

[165]https://bit.ly/3tQ2nO3
[166]https://bit.ly/425WXuH
[167]https://bit.ly/3StsfHt
[168]https://mzl.la/3aTGuQz

- Read more about faking a remote API with JavaScript[169].
  - Read more about using mock data in React[170].
- Optional: Leave feedback for this section[171].

Interview Questions:

- Question: Why is handling asynchronous data common in React applications?
  - Answer: Client-side React applications often fetch data from remote sources.
- Question: What is the typical approach for rendering components before data fetching in React?
  - Answer: Components are often rendered before initiating data fetching, and conditional rendering or placeholder content is used until the data arrives.
- Question: How can you simulate asynchronous data fetching in React using sample data?
  - Answer: Simulating asynchronous data involves using functions that return promises, resolving with sample data, and later replacing it with real data.
- Question: What is the purpose of promises in handling asynchronous data in React?
  - Answer: Promises are used to manage asynchronous operations, allowing components to wait for data resolution before rendering.
- Question: Why is asynchronous data fetching essential for responsive user interfaces in React?
  - Answer: Asynchronous data fetching prevents blocking the UI, ensuring responsiveness, and enabling the display of updated information when available.
- Question: Can you replace simulated sample data with real data fetched from a remote API in React?
  - Answer: Yes, after simulating asynchronous data with sample data, it can be replaced seamlessly with real data fetched from a remote API.
- Question: What is the significance of using the useState hook when dealing with asynchronous data in React?
  - Answer: useState allows components to manage state changes, including loading states and the updated data received asynchronously.
- Question: How does React ensure that components re-render when asynchronous data arrives?
  - Answer: React's state management ensures that when asynchronous data arrives and state is updated, components re-render to reflect the new data.

---

[169]https://www.robinwieruch.de/javascript-fake-api/
[170]https://www.robinwieruch.de/react-mock-data/
[171]https://forms.gle/sfQcc477xmgGRLyB7

React Conditional Rendering

We are set to introduce a new feature associated with the recently introduced asynchronous data handling. In a genuine application, users typically receive feedback, such as a loading spinner, while data is being loaded. In this section, our goal is to implement this feedback mechanism. Feel free to attempt implementing it independently, and later, you can refer to the book to compare your solution with the provided implementation.

Task: It takes some time to load the sample data from the promise. During this time, a user should be presented with a loading indicator in its simplest form (e.g. text which says "Loading …"). Once the data arrived asynchronously, hide the loading indicator.

Optional Hints:

- In order to show a loading indicator, one would need to introduce a new stateful value. A boolean called isLoading may be the best solution.
- When the side-effect which loads the data kicks in, set the stateful boolean to true. Once the data loaded, set the stateful boolean to false again.
- In JSX, show a "Loading …" text conditionally when the isLoading boolean is set to true.

A **conditional rendering** in React always happens if we have to render different JSX based on information (e.g. state, props). Dealing with asynchronous data is a good use case for making use of conditional rendering. For example, when the application initializes for the first time, there is no data to start with. Next, we are loading data and eventually, we have the data at our hands to display it. Sometimes the data fetching fails and we receive an error instead. So there are lots of things to cover for us as developers.

Fortunately, some aspects are already handled. For example, because the initial state is an empty list [] instead of null, concerns about breaking the application when filtering or mapping over this list are alleviated. Yet, certain aspects still need attention. Consider the absence of a loading state to provide users with feedback on pending data requests. Introducing a new stateful value can address this, allowing us to set the state accordingly when data is being fetched:

src/App.jsx

```
const App = () => {
  ...

  const [stories, setStories] = React.useState([]);
  const [isLoading, setIsLoading] = React.useState(false);

  React.useEffect(() => {
    setIsLoading(true);

    getAsyncStories().then((result) => {
```

```
    setStories(result.data.stories);
    setIsLoading(false);
  });
}, []);


...
};
```

The boolean should be toggled properly now. What's missing is showing the user the loading indicator. A straightforward approach would be using an early return in the App component:

src/App.jsx

```
const App = () => {
  ...

  if (isLoading) {
    return <p>Loading ...</p>;
  }

  return (
    <div>
      ...
    </div>
  );
};
```

However, this way *only* the loading indicator would render and nothing else. Instead, we want to inline the loading indicator within the JSX to either show the loading indicator or the List component. Using an if-else statement inlined in JSX is not encouraged though due to JSX's limitations here. (You can try it as exercise though.) However, you can use a ternary operator[172] instead and produce a **conditional rendering** in JSX this way:

---
[172]https://mzl.la/3vAPKCL

src/App.jsx

```
const App = () => {
  ...

  return (
    <div>

      ...

      <hr />

      {isLoading ? (
        <p>Loading ...</p>
      ) : (
        <List
          list={searchedStories}
          onRemoveItem={handleRemoveStory}
        />
      )}
    </div>
  );
};
```

That's already it. You are rendering conditionally a loading indicator or the List component based on a stateful boolean. Let's move on by implementing error handling for the asynchronous data too. An error doesn't happen in our simulated environment, but there could be errors if we start fetching data from a remote API. Therefore, introduce another state for error handling and handle it in the promise's catch() block when resolving the promise:

src/App.jsx

```
const App = () => {
  ...

  const [stories, setStories] = React.useState([]);
  const [isLoading, setIsLoading] = React.useState(false);
  const [isError, setIsError] = React.useState(false);

  React.useEffect(() => {
    setIsLoading(true);

    getAsyncStories()
      .then((result) => {
        setStories(result.data.stories);
```

```
        setIsLoading(false);
      })
      .catch(() => setIsError(true));
  }, []);


  ...
};
```

Next, give the user feedback in case something goes wrong with another conditional rendering. This time, it's either rendering something or nothing. So instead of having a ternary operator where one side returns null, use the logical && operator as shorthand:

src/App.jsx

```
const App = () => {
  ...

  return (
    <div>
      ...

      <hr />

      {isError && <p>Something went wrong ...</p>}

      {isLoading ? (
        <p>Loading ...</p>
      ) : (
        ...
      )}
    </div>
  );
};
```

In JavaScript, a true && 'Hello World' always evaluates to 'Hello World'. A false && 'Hello World' always evaluates to false. In React, we can use this behaviour to our advantage. If the condition is true, the expression after the logical && operator will be the output. If the condition is false, React ignores it and skips the expression. Using expression && JSX is more concise than using expression ? JSX : null.

Conditional rendering is not just for asynchronous data though. The simplest example of conditional rendering is a boolean state that's toggled with a button. If the boolean flag is true, render something, if it is false, don't render anything. Knowing about this feature in React can be quite powerful, because it gives you the ability to conditionally render JSX. It's yet another tool in React to make your UI more dynamic. And as we've discovered, it's often necessary for more complex control flows like asynchronous data.

Exercises:

- Compare your source code against the author's source code[173].
  - Recap all the source code changes from this section[174].
  - Optional: If you are using TypeScript, check out the author's source code here[175].
- Read more about conditional rendering in React[176].
- Optional: Leave feedback for this section[177].

Interview Questions:

- Question: Why didn't we need a conditional rendering for the empty `stories` before they get fetched from the fake API?
  - Answer: The `stories` are mapped as list in the List component by using the `map()` method. When mapping over a list, the `map()` method returns for every item a modified version (in our case JSX). If there are no items in the list, the `map()` method will return nothing. Therefore we do not need a conditional rendering here.
- Question: What would happen if the initial state of `stories` would be set to `null` instead of `[]`?
  - Answer: Then we would need a conditional rendering in the List component, because calling `map()` on `null` would throw an exception.
- Question: How can you conditionally render content based on state using useState?
  - Answer: Use conditional statements (e.g., if or ternary operator) in JSX based on the state value.
- Question: Can you use useState (or other hooks) inside conditional statements or loops?
  - Answer: No, hooks must be used at the top level of a function component, not within conditions or loops.
- Question: Why is conditional rendering often employed when handling asynchronous data in React?
  - Answer: Conditional rendering helps manage the UI display based on the state of asynchronous data, showing loading indicators or actual content as needed.
- Question: How do you handle loading states while waiting for asynchronous data in React?
  - Answer: Loading states are managed using conditional rendering or state variables, indicating to users that data is being fetched.
- Question: Can you handle errors during asynchronous data fetching in React?
  - Answer: Yes, error handling mechanisms, such as try...catch blocks or .catch with promises, can be implemented to manage errors during data fetching.

---

[173]https://bit.ly/3u1f2h5
[174]https://bit.ly/3tUXbIF
[175]https://bit.ly/3Ss5RP1
[176]https://www.robinwieruch.de/conditional-rendering-react/
[177]https://forms.gle/kHLAXtMaKsTFtWjY9

React Advanced State

All state management in this application makes heavy use of React's useState Hook. On the other hand, React's **useReducer Hook** enables one to use more sophisticated state management for complex state structures and transitions. Since the knowledge about reducers in JavaScript splits the community in half, we won't cover the basics here. However, if you haven't heard about reducers before, check out this guide about reducers in JavaScript[178].

In this section, we will move the stateful stories from React's useState hook to React's useReducer hook. Using useReducer over useState makes sense as soon as multiple stateful values are dependent on each other or related to one domain. For example, stories, isLoading, and error are all related to the data fetching. In a more abstract version, all three could be properties in a complex object (e.g. data, isLoading, error) managed by a reducer instead. We will cover this in a later section. In this section, we will start to manage the stories and its state transitions in a reducer.

First, introduce a reducer function outside of your components. A reducer function always receives a state and an action. Based on these two arguments, a reducer always returns a new state:

src/App.jsx

```
const getAsyncStories = () =>
  new Promise((resolve) => ... );

const storiesReducer = (state, action) => {
  if (action.type === 'SET_STORIES') {
    return action.payload;
  } else {
    throw new Error();
  }
};
```

A reducer action is always associated with a type and as a best practice with a payload. If the type matches a condition in the reducer, return a new state based on incoming state and action. If it isn't covered by the reducer, throw an error to remind yourself that the implementation isn't covered. The storiesReducer function covers one type and then returns the payload of the incoming action without using the current state to compute the new state. The new state is therefore simply the payload.

In the App component, exchange useState for useReducer for managing the stories. The new hook receives a reducer function and an initial state as arguments and returns an array with two items. The first item is the *current state* and the second item is the *state updater function* (also called *dispatch function*):

---

[178]https://www.robinwieruch.de/javascript-reducer/

src/App.jsx

```
const App = () => {
  ...

  const [stories, dispatchStories] = React.useReducer(
    storiesReducer,
    []
  );

  ...
};
```

The new dispatch function can be used instead of the setStories function, which was previously returned from useState. Instead of setting the state explicitly with the state updater function from useState, the useReducer state updater function sets the state implicitly by dispatching an action for the reducer. The action comes with a type and an optional payload:

src/App.jsx

```
const App = () => {
  ...

  React.useEffect(() => {
    setIsLoading(true);

    getAsyncStories()
      .then((result) => {
        dispatchStories({
          type: 'SET_STORIES',
          payload: result.data.stories,
        });
        setIsLoading(false);
      })
      .catch(() => setIsError(true));
  }, []);

  const handleRemoveStory = (item) => {
    const newStories = stories.filter(
      (story) => item.objectID !== story.objectID
    );

    dispatchStories({
      type: 'SET_STORIES',
```

```
      payload: newStories,
    });
  };


  . . .

};
```

The application appears the same in the browser, though a reducer and React's useReducer hook are managing the state for the stories now. Let's bring the concept of a reducer to a minimal version by handling more than one state transition. If there is only one state transition, a reducer wouldn't make sense.

So far, the handleRemoveStory handler computes the new stories. It's valid to move this logic into the reducer function and manage the reducer with an action, which is another case for moving from imperative to declarative programming. Instead of doing it ourselves by saying *how it should be done*, we are telling the reducer *what to do*. Everything else is hidden in the reducer:

src/App.jsx

```
const App = () => {
  . . .

  const handleRemoveStory = (item) => {
    dispatchStories({
      type: 'REMOVE_STORY',
      payload: item,
    });
  };


  . . .

};
```

Now the reducer function has to cover this new case in a new conditional state transition. If the condition for removing a story is met, the reducer has all the implementation details needed to remove the story. The action gives all the necessary information (here an item's identifier) to remove the story from the current state and return a new list of filtered stories as state:

src/App.jsx

```
const storiesReducer = (state, action) => {
  if (action.type === 'SET_STORIES') {
    return action.payload;
  } else if (action.type === 'REMOVE_STORY') {
    return state.filter(
      (story) => action.payload.objectID !== story.objectID
    );
  } else {
    throw new Error();
  }
};
```

All these if-else statements will eventually clutter when adding more state transitions into one reducer function. Refactoring it to a switch statement for all the state transitions makes it more readable and is seen as a best practice in the React community:

src/App.jsx

```
const storiesReducer = (state, action) => {
  switch (action.type) {
    case 'SET_STORIES':
      return action.payload;
    case 'REMOVE_STORY':
      return state.filter(
        (story) => action.payload.objectID !== story.objectID
      );
    default:
      throw new Error();
  }
};
```

What we've covered is a minimal version of a reducer in JavaScript and its usage in React with the help of React's useReducer Hook. The reducer covers two state transitions, shows how to compute the current state and action into a new state, and uses some business logic (removal of a story) for a state transition. Now we can set a list of stories as state for the asynchronously arriving data and remove a story from the list of stories with just one state managing reducer and its associated useReducer hook. To fully grasp the concept of reducers in JavaScript and the usage of React's useReducer Hook, visit the linked resources in the exercises. We will continue expanding our implementation of a reducer in the next section.

Exercises:

- Compare your source code against the author's source code[179].
    - Recap all the source code changes from this section[180].
    - Optional: If you are using TypeScript, check out the author's source code here[181].
- Read more about reducers and useReducer in React[182].
- Extract the action types `'SET_STORIES'` and `'REMOVE_STORY'` as variables and reuse them in the reducer and the dispatch functions. This way, you will avoid introducing typos in your action types.
- Optional: Leave feedback for this section[183].

Interview Questions:

- Question: What is useReducer in React?
    - Answer: useReducer is a React hook that manages complex state logic in function components by dispatching actions to update state.
- Question: How does useReducer differ from useState in React?
    - Answer: While useState is simpler for managing individual state variables, useReducer is more suitable for complex state logic where multiple values depend on each other.
- Question: What is the basic structure of the useReducer hook?
    - Answer: It returns the current state and a dispatch function for triggering state updates, taking a reducer function and an initial state as arguments.
- Question: What is a reducer function in useReducer?
    - Answer: The reducer function is responsible for specifying how the state should change in response to dispatched actions, based on the current state and the action.
- Question: How is state updated using useReducer?
    - Answer: State is updated by dispatching actions, and the reducer function determines the new state based on the current state and the action type.
- Question: Can useReducer replace all use cases of useState in React?
    - Answer: While useReducer is powerful, it's not necessary for all scenarios. useState is simpler and more suitable for managing individual state variables.

---

[179]https://bit.ly/48GEXd8
[180]https://bit.ly/3UbjXqx
[181]https://bit.ly/3OwtVie
[182]https://www.robinwieruch.de/react-usereducer-hook/
[183]https://forms.gle/tNqqVynwQV9Ym9u68

React Impossible States

Perhaps you've noticed a disconnect between the single states in the App component when using multiple of React's useState Hooks. Technically, all states related to the asynchronous data belong together, which doesn't only include the stories as actual data, but also their loading and error states. That's where one reducer and React's useReducer Hook come into play to manage domain related states. But why should we care?

There is nothing wrong with multiple useState hooks in one React component. Be wary once you see multiple state updater functions in a row, however. These conditional states can lead to **impossible states** and undesired behavior in the UI. Try changing your pseudo data fetching function to the following implementation to simulate an error and thus our implementation of error handling:

src/**App.jsx**

```
const getAsyncStories = () =>
  new Promise((resolve, reject) => setTimeout(reject, 2000));
```

The impossible state happens when an error occurs for the asynchronous data. The state for the error is set, but the state for the loading indicator isn't revoked. In the UI, this would lead to an infinite loading indicator and an error message, though it may be better to show the error message only and hide the loading indicator. Impossible states are not easy to spot, which makes them infamous for causing bugs in the UI. You could go on and try yourself to fix this bug.

Fortunately, we can improve our chances of not dealing with such bugs by moving states that belong together from multiple useState (and useReducer) hooks into a single useReducer hook. Take the following hooks:

src/**App.jsx**

```
const App = () => {
  ...

  const [stories, dispatchStories] = React.useReducer(
    storiesReducer,
    []
  );
  const [isLoading, setIsLoading] = React.useState(false);
  const [isError, setIsError] = React.useState(false);

  ...
};
```

And merge them into one useReducer hook for a unified state management which encompasses a more complex state object and eventually more complex state transitions:

src/App.jsx

```
const App = () => {
  ...

  const [stories, dispatchStories] = React.useReducer(
    storiesReducer,
    { data: [], isLoading: false, isError: false }
  );

  ...
};
```

Since we cannot use the state updater functions from React's useState Hooks anymore, everything related to asynchronous data fetching must use the new dispatch function for the state transitions. The most straightforward approach is exchanging the state updater function with the dispatch function. Then the dispatch function receives a distinct type and a payload. The latter resembles the same payload that we would have used to update the state with a state updater function:

src/App.jsx

```
const App = () => {
  ...

  const [stories, dispatchStories] = React.useReducer(
    storiesReducer,
    { data: [], isLoading: false, isError: false }
  );

  React.useEffect(() => {
    dispatchStories({ type: 'STORIES_FETCH_INIT' });

    getAsyncStories()
      .then((result) => {
        dispatchStories({
          type: 'STORIES_FETCH_SUCCESS',
          payload: result.data.stories,
        });
      })
      .catch(() =>
        dispatchStories({ type: 'STORIES_FETCH_FAILURE' })
      );
  }, []);
```

```
    ...
};
```

We changed two things for the reducer function. First, we introduced new types when we called the dispatch function from the outside. Therefore we need to add new cases for state transitions. And second, we changed the state structure from an array to a complex object. Therefore we need to take the new complex object into account as incoming state and returned state:

src/App.jsx

```
const storiesReducer = (state, action) => {
  switch (action.type) {
    case 'STORIES_FETCH_INIT':
      return {
        ...state,
        isLoading: true,
        isError: false,
      };
    case 'STORIES_FETCH_SUCCESS':
      return {
        ...state,
        isLoading: false,
        isError: false,
        data: action.payload,
      };
    case 'STORIES_FETCH_FAILURE':
      return {
        ...state,
        isLoading: false,
        isError: true,
      };
    case 'REMOVE_STORY':
      return {
        ...state,
        data: state.data.filter(
          (story) => action.payload.objectID !== story.objectID
        ),
      };
    default:
      throw new Error();
  }
};
```

For every state transition, we return a *new state* object which contains all the key/value pairs from the *current state* object (via JavaScript's spread operator) and the new overwriting properties. For example, `STORIES_FETCH_FAILURE` sets the `isLoading` boolean to `false` and sets the `isError` boolean to `true`, while keeping all the the other state intact (e.g. `data` alias `stories`). That's how we get around the bug introduced earlier as impossible state since an error should set the loading boolean to `false`.

Observe how the `REMOVE_STORY` action changed as well. It operates on the `state.data`, and no longer just on the plain `state`. The state is a complex object with `data`, `isLoading`, and `error` states rather than just a list of stories. This has to be solved in the remaining code by addressing the state as object and not as array anymore:

src/App.jsx

```
const App = () => {
  ...

  const [stories, dispatchStories] = React.useReducer(
    storiesReducer,
    { data: [], isLoading: false, isError: false }
  );

  ...

  const searchedStories = stories.data.filter((story) =>
    story.title.toLowerCase().includes(searchTerm.toLowerCase())
  );

  return (
    <div>
      ...

      {stories.isError && <p>Something went wrong ...</p>}

      {stories.isLoading ? (
        <p>Loading ...</p>
      ) : (
        <List
          list={searchedStories}
          onRemoveItem={handleRemoveStory}
        />
      )}
    </div>
  );
};
```

Try to use the erroneous data fetching function again and check whether everything works as expected now:

src/App.jsx

```
const getAsyncStories = () =>
  new Promise((resolve, reject) => setTimeout(reject, 2000));
```

We moved from unreliable state transitions with multiple useState hooks to predictable state transitions with React's useReducer Hook. The state object managed by the reducer encapsulates everything related to the fetching of stories including loading and error states, but also implementation details like removing a story from the stories. We didn't get fully rid of impossible states, because it's still possible to leave out a crucial boolean flag like before, but we moved one step closer towards more predictable state management.

Exercises:

- Compare your source code against the author's source code[184].
  - Recap all the source code changes from this section[185].

  - Optional: If you are using TypeScript, check out the author's source code here[186].
- Read more about when to use useState or useReducer in React[187].
- Read more about deriving state from props in React[188].
- Optional: Leave feedback for this section[189].

Interview Questions:

- Question: What are "impossible states" in React?
  - Answer: "Impossible states" refer to combinations of state values that should never occur in a well-designed application.
- Question: Why is it important to handle impossible states in React applications?
  - Answer: Handling impossible states ensures that the application remains in a valid and predictable state, preventing unexpected behavior.
- Question: How can reducers help manage impossible states in React?
  - Answer: Reducers provide a controlled way to update state, allowing developers to enforce rules and avoid transitioning to impossible states.
- Question: How does centralized state management contribute to handling impossible states?
  - Answer: Centralized state management through reducers allows for consistent validation and state updates, reducing the risk of impossible states across components.

---

[184]https://bit.ly/3SlNaO4
[185]https://bit.ly/4b2GkEh
[186]https://bit.ly/42nPpE1
[187]https://www.robinwieruch.de/react-usereducer-vs-usestate/
[188]https://www.robinwieruch.de/react-derive-state-props/
[189]https://forms.gle/XWTJS65iu6WkiZMCA

Data Fetching with React

We set everything up for asynchronous data fetching React. However, we are still using pseudo data coming from a promise we set up ourselves for a fake API. Still, all lessons up to now about asynchronous React and advanced state management were preparing us to fetch data from a real remote third-party API. In this section, we will use the informative Hacker News API[190] to request popular tech stories.

If you are familiar how to fetch data in JavaScript, you can try to accomplish the following task yourself and check later the implementation from the book. However, do not hesitate to continue with the book, because this is a tough task.

Task: The application uses asynchronous yet pseudo data from a promise (fake API). Instead of using the `getAsyncStories()` function, use the Hacker News API to fetch the data.

Optional Hints:

- Use this `https://hn.algolia.com/api/v1/search?query=React` API endpoint of the Hacker News API.
- Remove the `initialStories` variable, because this data will come from the API.
- Use the browser's native fetch API[191] to perform the request.
- Note: A successful or erroneous request uses the same implementation logic that we already have in place.

We start with a great foundation for fetching asynchronous data, because everything is already in place. The only thing that keeps us away from the solution is using sample data instead of real world data. Therefore, the next code snippet shows everything you need to change to connect to a remote API. Instead of using the `initialStories` array and `getAsyncStories` function, which can be removed now, we will fetch the data directly from the API:

src/App.jsx

```
// A
const API_ENDPOINT = 'https://hn.algolia.com/api/v1/search?query=';

const App = () => {
  ...

  React.useEffect(() => {
    dispatchStories({ type: 'STORIES_FETCH_INIT' });

    fetch(`${API_ENDPOINT}react`) // B
      .then((response) => response.json()) // C
```

---

[190]https://hn.algolia.com/api
[191]https://mzl.la/2Z1kyjU

```
      .then((result) => {
        dispatchStories({
          type: 'STORIES_FETCH_SUCCESS',
          payload: result.hits, // D
        });
      })
      .catch(() =>
        dispatchStories({ type: 'STORIES_FETCH_FAILURE' })
      );
  }, []);

  ...
};
```

First, the API_ENDPOINT (A) is used to fetch popular tech stories for a certain query (a search term). In this case, we fetch stories about React (B). Second, the native browser's fetch API[192] is used to make this request (B). For the fetch API, the response needs to be translated into JSON (C). Finally, the returned result has a different data structure (D), which we send as payload to our component's state reducer.

In the previous code example, we used JavaScript's Template Literals[193] for a string interpolation. When this feature wasn't available in JavaScript, we'd have used the + operator on strings instead:

Code Playground

```
const greeting = 'Hello';

// + operator
const welcome = greeting + ' React';
console.log(welcome);
// Hello React

// template literals
const anotherWelcome = `${greeting} React`;
console.log(anotherWelcome);
// Hello React
```

Check your browser to see stories related to the initial query fetched from the Hacker News API. Since we used the same data structure for the sample stories, we didn't need to change anything in the Item component. It's still possible to filter the stories after fetching them with the search feature, because they still have a title property. We will change this behavior in one of the next sections though.

---

[192]https://mzl.la/2Z1kyjU
[193]https://mzl.la/3jlcVfn

Exercises:

- Compare your source code against the author's source code[194].
  - Recap all the source code changes from this section[195].
  - Optional: If you are using TypeScript, check out the author's source code here[196].
- Read through Hacker News[197] and its API[198].
- Optional: Read more about JavaScript's Template Literals[199].
- Optional: Leave feedback for this section[200].

Interview Questions:

- Question: Why is fetching data from APIs common in React applications?
  - Answer: Fetching data from APIs allows React applications to dynamically retrieve and display information from external sources.
- Question: What is the purpose of the useEffect hook in React when working with APIs?
  - Answer: useEffect is used to perform side effects, such as data fetching, in function components. It ensures that the effect runs after rendering.
- Question: How do you handle asynchronous API calls in React components?
  - Answer: Asynchronous API calls are typically handled using async/await syntax or promises within the useEffect hook.
- Question: Can you perform cleanup operations after API requests using useEffect in React?
  - Answer: Yes, useEffect allows for cleanup operations, like canceling pending requests or clearing subscriptions, by returning a cleanup function.
- Question: What is the purpose of the second argument (dependency array) in useEffect when working with APIs?
  - Answer: The dependency array controls when the effect runs. Specifying dependencies ensures that the effect is re-executed only when those dependencies change.
- Question: How do you handle errors during API requests in React?
  - Answer: Errors during API requests can be handled using try...catch blocks, .catch with promises, or by setting error state variables.
- Question: What is the significance of state management when working with API data in React?
  - Answer: State management allows React components to store and update data retrieved from APIs, triggering re-renders when necessary.
- Question: Can you explain the concept of debouncing API requests in React?
  - Answer: Debouncing involves delaying the execution of API requests to reduce the number of requests made within a short time, typically to enhance performance and avoid rate limits.
- Question: Why is it important to handle loading states when making API requests in React?
  - Answer: Handling loading states provides feedback to users while data is being fetched, enhancing the user experience and indicating ongoing background processes.

---

[194]https://bit.ly/3O6YxXD
[195]https://bit.ly/3vErwvF
[196]https://bit.ly/3SztLZ0
[197]https://news.ycombinator.com
[198]https://hn.algolia.com/api
[199]https://mzl.la/3jlcVfn
[200]https://forms.gle/hoJxjjpoZQGCS7Vp9

Data Re-Fetching in React

Now, we have data retrieved from a remote API, providing a more engaging environment compared to sample data. If you launched your application after the previous section, you might have sensed that it lacks completeness. Since we fetch data with a predefined query (in this case: `'react'`), we consistently see stories related to "React." Despite having a search feature, it can only filter existing stories. Therefore, the search feature is termed a client-side search because it operates solely on the available data, without interacting with the remote API.

While a client-side search only filters the stories that are available on the client (after the initial data fetching), a server-side search would allow us to get data from the remote API based on the search term. Essentially client-side and server-side searching differ in where the search operation takes place. Client-side searching occurs on the user's device, providing fast responses but may be less suitable for large datasets. Server-side searching happens on the server, better suited for large datasets but may result in slower user response times due to server round-trips. The choice depends on factors like dataset size, search complexity, and performance considerations. In this section, we want to change the client-side search to a server-side search. Try to tackle the following task yourself again before continuing to read the book.

Task: The search feature is a client-side search, because it filters only the data that's already there. Instead it should be possible to use the search to fetch data related to the search term.

Optional Hints:

- The calculated value `searchedStories` can be omitted as we anticipate filtered data directly from the API.
- In the data retrieval process, replace the hardcoded `'react'` with the dynamic `searchTerm`.
- Address the edge case where `searchTerm` is an empty string.

There are not many steps involved to migrate the application from a client-side to a server-side search. First, remove `searchedStories` because we will receive the stories filtered by search term from the API. Pass only the regular stories to the List component:

src/App.jsx

```
const App = () => {
  ...

  return (
    <div>
      ...

      {stories.isLoading ? (
        <p>Loading ...</p>
      ) : (
```

```
          <List list={stories.data} onRemoveItem={handleRemoveStory} />
        )}
      </div>
    );
};
```

And second, instead of using the hardcoded search term (here: `'react'`), use the actual `searchTerm` from the component's state. Afterward, every time a user searches for something via the input field, the `searchTerm` will be used to request these kind of stories from the remote API. In addition, you need to deal with the edge case if `searchTerm` is an empty string, which means preventing a request from being fired:

src/App.jsx

```
const App = () => {
  ...

  React.useEffect(() => {
    if (searchTerm === '') return;

    dispatchStories({ type: 'STORIES_FETCH_INIT' });

    fetch(`${API_ENDPOINT}${searchTerm}`)
      .then((response) => response.json())
      .then((result) => {
        dispatchStories({
          type: 'STORIES_FETCH_SUCCESS',
          payload: result.hits,
        });
      })
      .catch(() =>
        dispatchStories({ type: 'STORIES_FETCH_FAILURE' })
      );
  }, []);

  ...
};
```

There is one crucial piece missing now. While the initial data fetching respects the `searchTerm` (here: `'React'` which is set as initial state), the `searchTerm` is not respected when it is changed via a user typing into the input field. If you inspect the dependency array of our `useEffect` hook, you will see that it's empty. This means the side-effect only renders for the initial rendering of the App component. If we would want to run the side-effect also when the `searchTerm` changes, we would have to include it in the dependency array:

src/App.jsx

```
const App = () => {
  ...

  React.useEffect(() => {
    // if `searchTerm` is not present
    // e.g. null, empty string, undefined
    // do nothing
    // more generalized condition than searchTerm === ''

    if (!searchTerm) return;

    dispatchStories({ type: 'STORIES_FETCH_INIT' });

    fetch(`${API_ENDPOINT}${searchTerm}`)
      .then((response) => response.json())
      .then((result) => {
        dispatchStories({
          type: 'STORIES_FETCH_SUCCESS',
          payload: result.hits,
        });
      })
      .catch(() =>
        dispatchStories({ type: 'STORIES_FETCH_FAILURE' })
      );
  }, [searchTerm]);

  ...
};
```

We've transitioned the feature from a client-side search to a server-side search. Instead of filtering a predefined list of stories on the client, the searchTerm is now utilized to retrieve a server-side filtered list. Server-side searching occurs not only during the initial data fetch but also when the searchTerm undergoes changes. The search feature is now entirely server-side.

Note: However, re-fetching data with every keystroke isn't optimal, as this implementation puts strain on the API with frequent requests. Excessive requests may lead to API errors due to rate limiting, a measure many APIs employ to protect against a high volume of requests (e.g., allowing only X requests in 1 minute). We plan to address this issue soon.

Exercises:

- Compare your source code against the author's source code[201].
  - Recap all the source code changes from this section[202].
  - Optional: If you are using TypeScript, check out the author's source code here[203].
- Optional: Leave feedback for this section[204].

Interview Questions:

- Question: What is client-side searching?
  - Answer: Client-side searching involves filtering and manipulating data on the user's device or browser.
- Question: How does client-side searching impact performance?
  - Answer: It can offer fast response times but may be limited by the amount of data that needs to be loaded from the server.
- Question: What is server-side searching?
  - Answer: Server-side searching entails sending search queries to the server, where the data is filtered, and the results are returned to the client.
- Question: When is server-side searching preferred?
  - Answer: Server-side searching is preferable for large datasets or when complex search logic and data reside on the server.
- Question: What are potential drawbacks of client-side searching?
  - Answer: Limitations may arise with large datasets, slower initial page loads, and the need to load extensive data to the client.
- Question: What is the impact of frequent API requests in client-side searching?
  - Answer: Frequent requests can stress the API, potentially leading to errors, especially if the API employs rate limiting measures.
- Question: How can the performance issue of frequent API requests be addressed?
  - Answer: Implementing debouncing or throttling techniques can mitigate the impact of frequent API requests and prevent overloading the server.

---

[201]https://bit.ly/3vF23lz
[202]https://bit.ly/3U4PB8Q
[203]https://bit.ly/492rkVN
[204]https://forms.gle/ywE4bFy6D2HSG8Rd7

Memoized Functions in React (Advanced)

Most often, functions defined in React components serve as event handlers. However, given that a React component is essentially a function itself, you can also declare functions, function expressions, and arrow function expressions within a component. This section introduces the concept of a memoized function using React's useCallback Hook.

To begin, we'll proactively refactor the code to incorporate a memoized function, followed by detailed explanations. The refactoring involves transferring all data fetching logic from the side-effect into an arrow function expression (A). This new function is then encapsulated within React's useCallback hook (B) and subsequently invoked within the useEffect hook (C):

src/App.jsx

```
const App = () => {
  ...

  // A
  const handleFetchStories = React.useCallback(() => { // B
    if (!searchTerm) return;

    dispatchStories({ type: 'STORIES_FETCH_INIT' });

    fetch(`${API_ENDPOINT}${searchTerm}`)
      .then((response) => response.json())
      .then((result) => {
        dispatchStories({
          type: 'STORIES_FETCH_SUCCESS',
          payload: result.hits,
        });
      })
      .catch(() =>
        dispatchStories({ type: 'STORIES_FETCH_FAILURE' })
      );
  }, [searchTerm]); // E

  React.useEffect(() => {
    handleFetchStories(); // C
  }, [handleFetchStories]); // D

  ...
};
```

At its core, the application behaves the same, because we have only extracted a new function from

React's useEffect Hook. Instead of using the data fetching logic directly in the side-effect, we made it available as a function for the entire application. The benefit: reusability. The data fetching can be used by other parts of the application by calling this new function. However, we have used React's useCallback Hook to wrap the extracted function, so let's explore why it's needed here. React's useCallback Hook creates a memoized function every time its dependency array (E) changes. As a result, the useEffect hook runs again (C), because it depends on the new function (D):

Visualization

```
1. change: searchTerm (cause: user interaction)
2. change: handleFetchStories (cause: changed searchTerm)
3. run: side-effect (cause: changed handleFetchStories)
```

If we would leave out React's useCallback Hook and only define the new handleFetchStories event handler without it, a new handleFetchStories function would be created each time the App component re-renders, and would be executed in the useEffect hook to fetch data. The fetched data is then stored as state in the component. Then, because the state of the component changed, the component re-renders and creates a new handleFetchStories function. The side-effect would be triggered to fetch data, and we'd be stuck in an endless loop:

Visualization

```
1. define: handleFetchStories
2. run: side-effect
3. update: state
4. re-render: component
5. re-define: handleFetchStories
6. run: side-effect
...
```

You could try this infinite loop yourself by removing React's useCallback Hook, but be prepared for a crashing browser. After all, React's useCallback hook changes the function only when one of its values in the dependency array changes. That's when we want to trigger a re-fetch of the data, because the input field has new input and we want to see the new data displayed in our list.

By moving the data fetching function outside the React's useEffect Hook, it becomes reusable for other parts of the application. We won't use it just yet, but it is a good use case to understand the memoized functions in React. Now the useEffect hook runs implicitly when the searchTerm changes, because the handleFetchStories is re-defined each time the searchTerm changes. Since the useEffect hook depends on the handleFetchStories, the side-effect for data fetching runs again.

Exercises:

- Compare your source code against the author's source code[205].

---

[205]https://bit.ly/422ZA0k

- Recap all the source code changes from this section[206].
- Optional: If you are using TypeScript, check out the author's source code here[207].
- Read more about React's useCallback Hook[208].
- Optional: Leave feedback for this section[209].

Interview Questions:

- Question: What is the purpose of the useCallback hook in React?
  - Answer: useCallback is used to memoize functions in React, preventing unnecessary re-creations of functions on re-renders.
- Question: When should you use useCallback in a React component?
  - Answer: Use useCallback when you want to memoize a function to optimize performance, especially in scenarios involving callback functions passed to child components.
- Question: What are the arguments of the useCallback hook?
  - Answer: The first argument is the function to be memoized, and the second argument is an array of dependencies that, when changed, trigger the creation of a new memoized function.
- Question: What happens if the dependencies array in useCallback is empty?
  - Answer: If the dependencies array is empty, the memoized function is created only once and remains the same throughout the component's lifecycle.

---

[206]https://bit.ly/3vFwrMT
[207]https://bit.ly/49Fo6Yj
[208]https://www.robinwieruch.de/react-usecallback-hook/
[209]https://forms.gle/HSX9aurgsf5j76HR9

Explicit Data Fetching with React

Re-fetching all data each time someone types in the input field isn't optimal. Since we're using a third-party API to fetch the data, its internals are out of our reach. Eventually, we will be confronted with rate limiting[210] which returns an error instead of data. To solve this problem, we will change the implementation details from implicit to explicit data (re-)fetching. In other words, the application will refetch data only if someone clicks a confirmation button.

Task: The server-side search executes every time a user types into the input field. The new implementation should only execute a search when a user clicks a confirmation button. As long as the button is not clicked, the search term can change but isn't executed as API request.

Optional Hints:

- Add a button element to confirm the search request.
- Create a stateful value for the confirmed search.
- The button's event handler sets confirmed search as state by using the current search term.
- Only when the new confirmed search is set as state, execute the side-effect to perform a server-side search.

What's important with this feature is that we need a state for the fluctuating `searchTerm` and a new state for the confirmed search. But first of all, create a new button element which confirms the search and executes the data request eventually:

src/App.jsx

```
const App = () => {
  ...

  return (
    <div>
      <h1>My Hacker Stories</h1>

      <InputWithLabel
        id="search"
        value={searchTerm}
        isFocused
        onInputChange={handleSearchInput}
      >
        <strong>Search:</strong>
      </InputWithLabel>

      <button
```

---
[210]https://bit.ly/2ZaJXI8

```
        type="button"
        disabled={!searchTerm}
        onClick={handleSearchSubmit}
      >
        Submit
      </button>

      ...

    </div>
  );
};
```

Second, we distinguish between the handler of the input field and the button. While the renamed handler of the input field still sets the stateful searchTerm, the new handler of the button sets the new stateful value called url which is derived from the *current* searchTerm and the static API endpoint as a new state:

src/App.jsx

```
const App = () => {
  const [searchTerm, setSearchTerm] = useStorageState(
    'search',
    'React'
  );

  const [url, setUrl] = React.useState(
    `${API_ENDPOINT}${searchTerm}`
  );

  ...

  const handleSearchInput = (event) => {
    setSearchTerm(event.target.value);
  };

  const handleSearchSubmit = () => {
    setUrl(`${API_ENDPOINT}${searchTerm}`);
  };

  ...

};
```

Third, instead of running the data fetching side-effect on every searchTerm change (which happens each time the input field's value changes like we have seen before), the new stateful `url` is used whenever a user changes it by confirming a search request when clicking the button:

src/App.jsx

```
const App = () => {

  ...

  const handleFetchStories = React.useCallback(() => {
    dispatchStories({ type: 'STORIES_FETCH_INIT' });

    fetch(url)
      .then((response) => response.json())
      .then((result) => {
        dispatchStories({
          type: 'STORIES_FETCH_SUCCESS',
          payload: result.hits,
        });
      })
      .catch(() =>
        dispatchStories({ type: 'STORIES_FETCH_FAILURE' })
      );
  }, [url]);

  React.useEffect(() => {
    handleFetchStories();
  }, [handleFetchStories]);

  ...

};
```

Before the `searchTerm` was used for two cases: updating the input field's state and activating the side-effect for fetching data. Now it's only used for the former. A second state called `url` got introduced for triggering the side-effect that fetches the data which only happens when a user clicks the confirmation button.

Exercises:

- Compare your source code against the author's source code[211].
  - Recap all the source code changes from this section[212].
  - Optional: If you are using TypeScript, check out the author's source code here[213].
- Optional: Leave feedback for this section[214].

[211]https://bit.ly/3Soxdqc
[212]https://bit.ly/3S3vJAo
[213]https://bit.ly/42tCHUa
[214]https://forms.gle/HuJDuVNZmEDbhGzU9

Interview Questions:

- Question: Why is `useState` instead of `useStorageState` used for the `url` state management?
  - Answer: We do not want to remember the `url` in the browser's local storage, because it's already derived from a static string (here: `API_ENDPOINT`) and the `searchTerm` which already comes from the browser's local storage.
- Question: Why is there no check for an empty `searchTerm` in the `handleFetchStories` function anymore?
  - Answer: Preventing a server-side search happens in the new button, because it gets disabled whenever there is no `searchTerm`.

Third-Party Libraries in React

We previously introduced the native fetch API (which the browser provides) to perform requests to the Hacker News API. However, not all browsers support this, especially the older ones. Also, once you start testing your application in a headless browser environment[215], issues can arise with the fetch API, because the actual browser is not there. There are a couple of ways to make fetch work in older browsers (polyfills[216]) and in tests (isomorphic fetch), but these concepts are a bit off-task for the purpose of this learning experience.

One alternative is to substitute the native fetch API with a stable library like axios[217], which performs asynchronous requests to remote APIs. In this section, we will discover how to substitute a library – a native API of the browser in this case – with another library from the npm registry.

If you know how to install axios via npm and use it as replacement for the browser's fetch API, go ahead and implement it yourself. Otherwise, the book will guide you through the implementation. First, install axios from the command line:

Command Line

```
npm install axios
```

Second, import axios in your App component's file:

src/App.jsx

```
import * as React from 'react';
import axios from 'axios';

...
```

You can use axios instead of fetch. Its usage looks almost identical to the native fetch API: It takes the URL as an argument and returns a promise. You don't have to transform the returned response to JSON anymore, since axios wraps the result into a data object in JavaScript for you. Just make sure to adapt your code to the returned data structure:

---

[215]https://bit.ly/3ncFfSs
[216]https://bit.ly/3ASC86Y
[217]https://bit.ly/3jjEupg

src/App.jsx

```
const App = () => {
  ...

  const handleFetchStories = React.useCallback(() => {
    dispatchStories({ type: 'STORIES_FETCH_INIT' });

    axios
      .get(url)
      .then((result) => {
        dispatchStories({
          type: 'STORIES_FETCH_SUCCESS',
          payload: result.data.hits,
        });
      })
      .catch(() =>
        dispatchStories({ type: 'STORIES_FETCH_FAILURE' })
      );
  }, [url]);

  ...
};
```

In this code, we call axios `axios.get()` for an explicit HTTP GET request[218], which is the same HTTP method we used by default with the browser's native fetch API. You can use other HTTP methods such as HTTP POST with `axios.post()` as well. We can see with these examples that axios is a powerful library for performing requests to remote APIs. I recommend it over the native fetch API when requests become complex, working with older browsers, or for testing.

Exercises:

- Compare your source code against the author's source code[219].
  - Recap all the source code changes from this section[220].
  - Optional: If you are using TypeScript, check out the author's source code here[221].
- Read more about popular libraries in React[222].
- Optional: Read more about axios[223].
- Optional: Leave feedback for this section[224].

---

[218]https://mzl.la/3n5kUyi
[219]https://bit.ly/3O8sXbU
[220]https://bit.ly/3vHe3mC
[221]https://bit.ly/3Ss6Yyb
[222]https://www.robinwieruch.de/react-libraries/
[223]https://bit.ly/3jjEupg
[224]https://forms.gle/wfDb7r5K4az3TiWN9

Interview Questions:

- Question: What is Axios in the context of React?
  - Answer: Axios is a popular JavaScript library for making HTTP requests, commonly used in React applications for data fetching.
- Question: How does Axios differ from the Fetch API in React?
  - Answer: Axios is a third-party library providing additional features and a more convenient API compared to the native Fetch API.
- Question: Why might you choose Axios over Fetch in a React project?
  - Answer: Axios offers features like automatic JSON parsing, request/response interceptors, and better browser support, making it a preferred choice for many developers.
- Question: How do you make a GET request using Axios in React?
  - Answer: Use axios.get(url) to make a GET request in React with Axios.
- Question: How is error handling done in Axios requests in React?
  - Answer: Axios provides a .catch() method to handle errors in the request.
- Question: What is the main advantage of using Fetch API in React?
  - Answer: The Fetch API is built into modern browsers, eliminating the need for additional dependencies and making it a lightweight choice for simple scenarios.

Async/Await in React

There is no way around asynchronous data when working on real world applications. There will always be a remote API that gives you data, whether it is on the frontend or backend, so you need to understand how to work with this data asynchronously. In our React application, we have started to resolve promises with then/catch blocks. However, in modern JavaScript (and therefore React), a more popular solution is using async/await.

If you are already familiar with async/await or you want to explore its usage[225] yourself, go ahead and change the code from using then/catch to async/await. If you have come this far, you could also consider compensating for the removal of the catch block for the error handling by using a try/catch block instead.

Let's continue with the task here. First, you would have to replace the then/catch syntax with the async/await syntax. The following refactoring of the handleFetchStories() function shows how to accomplish it without error handling:

src/App.jsx

```
const App = () => {
  ...

  const handleFetchStories = React.useCallback(async () => {
    dispatchStories({ type: 'STORIES_FETCH_INIT' });

    const result = await axios.get(url);

    dispatchStories({
      type: 'STORIES_FETCH_SUCCESS',
      payload: result.data.hits,
    });
  }, [url]);

  ...
};
```

To use async/await, our function requires the async keyword. Once you start using the await keyword on returned promises, everything reads like synchronous code. Actions after the await keyword are not executed until the promise resolves, meaning the code will wait. To include error handling as before, the try and catch blocks are there to help. If something goes wrong in the try block, the code will jump into the catch block to handle the error:

---

[225]https://mzl.la/3AWyWaw

src/App.jsx

```
const App = () => {
  ...

  const handleFetchStories = React.useCallback(async () => {
    dispatchStories({ type: 'STORIES_FETCH_INIT' });

    try {
      const result = await axios.get(url);

      dispatchStories({
        type: 'STORIES_FETCH_SUCCESS',
        payload: result.data.hits,
      });
    } catch {
      dispatchStories({ type: 'STORIES_FETCH_FAILURE' });
    }
  }, [url]);

  ...
};
```

After all, using async/await with try/catch over then/catch makes it often more readable, because we avoid using callback functions and instead try to make our code more readable in a synchronous way. However, using then/catch is fine too. In the end, the whole team working on a project should agree on one syntax.

Exercises:

- Compare your source code against the author's source code[226].
  - Recap all the source code changes from this section[227].
  - Optional: If you are using TypeScript, check out the author's source code here[228].
- Read more about data fetching in React[229].
- Optional: Leave feedback for this section[230].

---

[226]https://bit.ly/3S8xI6D
[227]https://bit.ly/42llSLf
[228]https://bit.ly/3wdPFJq
[229]https://www.robinwieruch.de/react-hooks-fetch-data/
[230]https://forms.gle/mtMmwrrsiwioZ8GH6

Interview Questions:

- Question: What is async/await?
  - Answer: async and await are keywords in JavaScript used for handling asynchronous operations in a synchronous-like manner, making code more readable.
- Question: How do you use async/await with a function in React?
  - Answer: Declare the function with the async keyword and use await within the function to handle promises.
- Question: What is the purpose of async functions in React?
  - Answer: async functions allow you to work with asynchronous code in a more readable and sequential manner, enhancing the handling of promises.
- Question: How do you handle errors with async/await in React?
  - Answer: Use a try/catch block to catch and handle errors in an async function.
- Question: How does async/await differ from using .then() with Promises in React?
  - Answer: async/await provides a more concise syntax, making asynchronous code look similar to synchronous code, compared to chaining .then().
- Question: Can you use async/await with the Fetch API in React?
  - Answer: Yes, async/await is commonly used with the Fetch API for asynchronous data fetching in React.
- Question: How do you handle multiple asynchronous operations with async/await in React?
  - Answer: Use Promise.all() to handle multiple asynchronous operations concurrently in an async function.

Forms in React

There is no modern application that doesn't use forms. A form is just a proper vehicle to submit data via a button from various input controls (e.g. input field, checkbox, radio button, slider). Earlier we introduced a new button to fetch data explicitly with a button click. We'll advance its use with a proper HTML form, which encapsulates the button and input field for the search term with its label.

Forms aren't much different in React's JSX than in HTML. We'll implement it in two refactoring steps with some HTML/JavaScript. First, wrap the input field and button into an HTML form element:

src/App.jsx

```
const App = () => {
  ...

  return (
    <div>
      <h1>My Hacker Stories</h1>

      <form onSubmit={handleSearchSubmit}>
        <InputWithLabel
          id="search"
          value={searchTerm}
          isFocused
          onInputChange={handleSearchInput}
        >
          <strong>Search:</strong>
        </InputWithLabel>

        <button type="submit" disabled={!searchTerm}>
          Submit
        </button>
      </form>

      <hr />

      ...
    </div>
  );
};
```

Instead of passing the `handleSearchSubmit()` handler to the button, it's used in the new form element's `onSubmit` attribute. The button receives a new `type` attribute called `submit`, which indicates that the form element's onSubmit handles the click and not the button. Next, since the handler is used for the form event, it executes preventDefault() additionally on React's synthetic event. This prevents the HTML form's native behavior which would lead to a browser reload:

src/App.jsx

```
const App = () => {
  ...

  const handleSearchSubmit = (event) => {
    setUrl(`${API_ENDPOINT}${searchTerm}`);

    event.preventDefault();
  };

  ...
};
```

Now we can execute the search feature with the keyboard's "Enter" key, because we are using a form instead of just a standalone button. In the next two steps, we will separate the whole form into a new SearchForm component. If you want to go ahead yourself, do not hesitate. Anyway, this is how the form can be extracted into its own component:

src/App.jsx

```
const SearchForm = ({
  searchTerm,
  onSearchInput,
  onSearchSubmit,
}) => (
  <form onSubmit={onSearchSubmit}>
    <InputWithLabel
      id="search"
      value={searchTerm}
      isFocused
      onInputChange={onSearchInput}
    >
      <strong>Search:</strong>
    </InputWithLabel>

    <button type="submit" disabled={!searchTerm}>
      Submit
    </button>
  </form>
);
```

The new component is instantiated in the App component. The App component still manages the state for the form though, because the state triggers the data request in the App component where the requested data will eventually get passed as props (here: stories.data) to the List component:

src/App.jsx

```
const App = () => {
  ...

  return (
    <div>
      <h1>My Hacker Stories</h1>

      <SearchForm
        searchTerm={searchTerm}
        onSearchInput={handleSearchInput}
        onSearchSubmit={handleSearchSubmit}
      />

      <hr />

      {stories.isError && <p>Something went wrong ...</p>}

      {stories.isLoading ? (
        <p>Loading ...</p>
      ) : (
        <List list={stories.data} onRemoveItem={handleRemoveStory} />
      )}
    </div>
  );
};
```

Forms aren't much different in React than in plain HTML. When we have input fields and a button to submit data from them, we can give our HTML more structure by wrapping it into a form element with a onSubmit attribute. The button that executes the submission therefore needs the "submit" type to refer the process to the form element's handler. After all, it makes it more accessible for keyboard users as well.

Exercises:

- Compare your source code against the author's source code[231].

---

[231]https://bit.ly/3u4ZHfi

- Recap all the source code changes from this section[232].
  - Optional: If you are using TypeScript, check out the author's source code here[233].
- Read more about forms in React[234].
- Try what happens without using `preventDefault`.
  - Read more about preventDefault for events in React[235].
- Optional: Leave feedback for this section[236].

Interview Questions:

- Questions: How do you handle form input in React?
  - Answers: In React, form input is typically managed using state. Each input field has a corresponding state variable, and the value of the input is set to the state.
- Questions: What is the purpose of the onChange event in React forms?
  - Answers: The onChange event is used to capture user input in real-time and update the state accordingly, ensuring the form reflects the latest input.
- Questions: How can you prevent the default form submission behavior in React?
  - Answers: Use the e.preventDefault() method within the form's submit handler to prevent the default form submission behavior.
- Questions: What is controlled and uncontrolled form input in React?
  - Answers: Controlled form input is when React state manages the input value. Uncontrolled input is when the DOM handles the input, and React does not track its state.
- Questions: How do you perform form validation in React?
  - Answers: Form validation in React is typically done by checking the input values against certain conditions or using validation libraries. The onSubmit handler is a common place to implement validation.
- Questions: What is the purpose of the value attribute in form inputs?
  - Answers: The value attribute sets the initial value of a form input and ensures that the input is controlled by React state.
- Questions: How can you handle multiple form inputs with a single onChange handler in React?
  - Answers: Use the name attribute on each input field and access the corresponding value using event.target.name in the onChange handler.
- Questions: What is the role of the onSubmit event in React forms?
  - Answers: The onSubmit event is triggered when the form is submitted. It's where you handle form validation, data processing, or any other actions related to the form submission.

---

[232]https://bit.ly/3SpINjZ
[233]https://bit.ly/42qnJ18
[234]https://www.robinwieruch.de/react-form/
[235]https://www.robinwieruch.de/react-preventdefault/
[236]https://forms.gle/d14Mf7WzetP25jxq5

A Roadmap for React

So far, you have learned everything that you need to know about React's fundamentals. With this knowledge, you *could* take a break from this book and create a minimal React application yourself. There will for sure be questions popping up, but you can always seek answers by going through the fundamentals of this book again. After all, learning React.js (and any other programming language, framework, library) is best done by getting your hands dirty. My favorite approach: Learn the fundamentals, learn how to connect to an API, find an API that delivers data which aligns with your personal interests, and build something with it! Fortifying your knowledge of the fundamentals is key to what comes next.

Continuing from here, there are several paths you can take for your learning experience. First of all, you can continue reading this book. At its core, the next sections will primarily touch three aspects: advanced features of React, organizational topics for every React project, and React's ecosystem. You will learn about topics such as performance optimizations, folder/file structures of a React project, static types with TypeScript, and styling in React. However, in my opinion, I kept the selection to a non-overwhelming minimum, because otherwise this book would be a never ending story. If you have the desire to dive deeper into various subjects though, I can give you the following material below.

React's ecosystem is huge. Every year I sum up all the essential yet popular libraries[237] that can be used in React for various aspects. You can poke around in the list and try different libraries that could improve your own project. For some of them I have written dedicated tutorial series too, such as React Router[238] and React Table Library[239]. While the former is the most popular routing library for React, the latter is a library which I open sourced myself to create data tables in React and which runs in production for several of my freelance clients.

Next there is one advanced feature in React that we didn't touch in the book and will not touch in the rest of it. I kept it outside because of one reason: it's an advanced feature which would bloat our minimal application without really showing what problem it solves. So it would end up being a premature optimization in the eyes of every intermediate developer or an obstacle in the eyes of every novice developer. However, you may come across it eventually, so I don't want you to miss it: React Context. If you want to learn about it, I highly recommend you to read more about React Context[240] and React's useContext Hook[241] in addition to actually using it for a more advanced pattern by combining multiple hooks in a real application[242] (recommended read).

---

[237]https://www.robinwieruch.de/react-libraries

[238]https://www.robinwieruch.de/react-router/

[239]https://www.robinwieruch.de/react-table-component/

[240]https://www.robinwieruch.de/react-context/

[241]https://www.robinwieruch.de/react-usecontext-hook/

[242]https://www.robinwieruch.de/react-state-usereducer-usestate-usecontext/

React comes with many patterns for components too. You have learned about component composition[243] and reusable components[244] already. If you haven't read the referenced tutorials about these patterns, I encourage you to catch up with them. There are more patterns though, and covering all of them here wouldn't give the patterns justice in a small application. That's why I covered them, e.g. React Render Prop Components[245] and React Higher-Order Components[246], extensively in other material of mine. With the succession of React Hooks though, these patterns are less used these days; however, in larger React applications you will most likely encounter them.

Furthermore, you have used Vite to bootstrap your project in this book. If you are interested in setting up a React project from scratch[247] yourself, by using tools such as Webpack and Babel which power JavaScript build pipelines, I encourage you to go through the process. You will learn lots about what's going on under the hood in a third-party tool like Vite.

Now we've reached the middle of the Road to React, and I hope you enjoyed reading it so far. In case you liked it, it would mean a lot to me if you would share the book with your friends who are interested in learning React. Also, a **review on** Amazon[248] or Goodreads[249] would be very much appreciated.

From here on, you can continue reading the book to learn about an opinionated selection of React's ecosystem, organizational recommendations, and more built-in features of React (e.g. performance optimizations). At the end of the book, you will find even more sections helping you to implement advanced features for your current React application. In summary, I hope all of the prior learnings, the referenced material, plus the following sections of the book help you to become a great React developer.

Important: The following chapters with their sections do not follow a linear path anymore. While all of them build up on the application that you have got right now, they will fork into different directions. You can try on your own to merge them all into your current application (which works most of the times, but not for the styling sections where you have to choose a path). If this gets too overwhelming, there are two alternatives to this approach:

1. Copy and paste the current application and use one copy for each individual path:
2. Read a chapter (path) with its sections (potential subpaths), apply the changes, and optionally revert the changes after the learning to start with a clean slate with the next chapter.

Let me summarize the paths you can with this book below:

- Styling in React: Each section in this chapter demonstrates an **alternative path**.
- React Maintenance: The chapter follows a **linear path** with its sections.

[243]https://www.robinwieruch.de/react-component-composition/
[244]https://www.robinwieruch.de/react-reusable-components/
[245]https://www.robinwieruch.de/react-render-props/
[246]https://www.robinwieruch.de/react-higher-order-components/
[247]https://www.robinwieruch.de/minimal-react-webpack-babel-setup/
[248]https://amzn.to/2JHlP42
[249]https://www.goodreads.com/book/show/37503118-the-road-to-learn-react

- TypeScript in React: The chapter follows a **linear path** with its sections.
- Testing in React: The chapter follows a **linear path** with its sections.
- React Project Structure: The chapter follows a **linear path** with its sections.
- Real World React (Advanced): The chapter follows a **linear path** with its sections.

All chapters will build upon your current application. No other chapter will inherit the changes from the other chapters though.

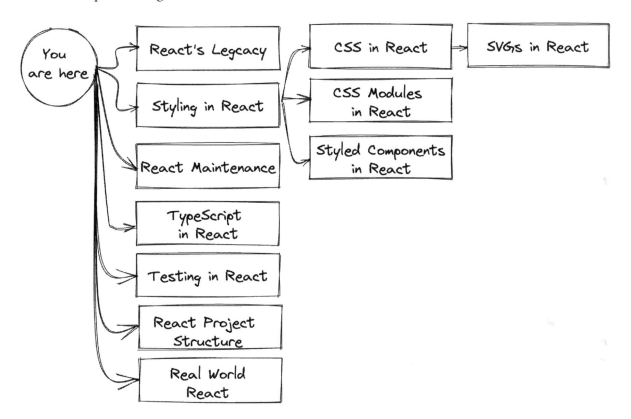

Styling in React

There are many ways to style a React application, and there are lengthy debates about the best **styling strategy** and **styling approach**. We'll go over a few of these strategies each representing one approach without giving them too much weight. There will be some pro and con arguments, but it's mostly a matter of what fits best for developers and their teams.

We will begin React styling with common CSS in React, but then explore two alternatives for more advanced **CSS-in-CSS** (with **CSS Modules**) and **CSS-in-JS** (with s**Styled Components**) strategies. CSS Modules and Styled Components are only two approaches out of many in both groups of strategies. We'll also cover how to include scalable vector graphics (SVGs), such as a logo or icons, in our React application.

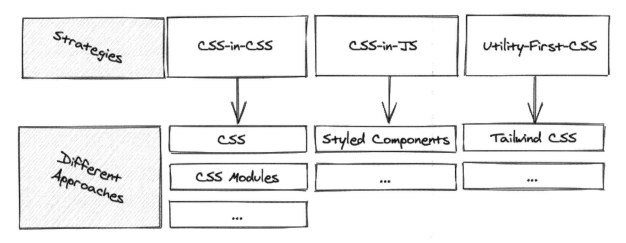

If you don't want to build common UI components (e.g. button, dialog, dropdown) from scratch, you can always pick a popular UI library suited for React[250], which provides these components by default. However, it is better for learning React if you try building these components before using a pre-built solution. As a result, we won't use any of the UI component libraries.

---

[250]https://www.robinwieruch.de/react-libraries/

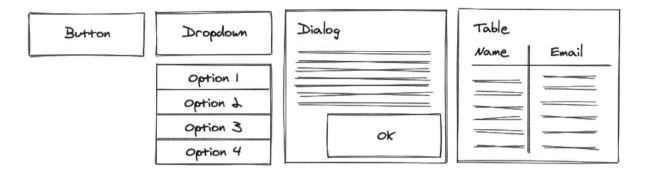

The following styling approaches and SVGs are mostly pre-configured in Vite. If you're in control of the build tools (e.g. Webpack) by having a custom setup, they might need to be configured to enable importing CSS or SVG files. Since we are using Vite, we can use these files right away. For example, in your *src/main.jsx* file, make sure to import the *src/index.css* file:

src/main.jsx

```
import React from 'react';
import ReactDOM from 'react-dom/client';
import App from './App';

import './index.css';

ReactDOM.createRoot(document.getElementById('root')).render(
  <React.StrictMode>
    <App />
  </React.StrictMode>
);
```

Use the following CSS in the *src/index.css* file for removing the margin and for using a standardized font with fallbacks:

src/index.css

```
body {
  margin: 0;
  font-family: -apple-system, BlinkMacSystemFont, 'Segoe UI', 'Roboto', 'Oxygen',
    'Ubuntu', 'Cantarell', 'Fira Sans', 'Droid Sans', 'Helvetica Neue',
    sans-serif;
  -webkit-font-smoothing: antialiased;
  -moz-osx-font-smoothing: grayscale;
}
```

Essentially you can declare all the CSS that should apply globally for your project in this file.

Exercises:

- Compare your source code against the author's source code[251].
  - Recap all the source code changes from this section[252].
- Read more about the different styling strategies and approaches in React[253].

---

[251]https://bit.ly/3xLnIXI
[252]https://bit.ly/3f2gJ5U
[253]https://www.robinwieruch.de/react-css-styling/

CSS in React

Common CSS in React is similar to the standard CSS you may have already learned. Each web application gives HTML elements a `class` (in React it's `className`) attribute that is styled via a CSS file:

src/App.jsx

```
const App = () => {

  ...

  return (
    <div className="container">
      <h1 className="headline-primary">My Hacker Stories</h1>

      <SearchForm
        searchTerm={searchTerm}
        onSearchInput={handleSearchInput}
        onSearchSubmit={handleSearchSubmit}
      />

      {stories.isError && <p>Something went wrong ...</p>}

      {stories.isLoading ? (
        <p>Loading ...</p>
      ) : (
        <List list={stories.data} onRemoveItem={handleRemoveStory} />
      )}
    </div>
  );
};
```

The `<hr />` was removed because the CSS handles the border in the next steps. We'll import the CSS file, which is done with the help of how Vite resolves imports:

src/App.jsx

```
import * as React from 'react';
import axios from 'axios';

import './App.css';
```

This CSS file will define the two (and more) CSS classes we used (and will use) in the App component. In your *src/App.css* file, define them like the following:

src/App.css

```css
.container {
  height: 100vw;
  padding: 20px;

  background: #83a4d4; /* fallback for old browsers */
  background: linear-gradient(to left, #b6fbff, #83a4d4);

  color: #171212;
}

.headline-primary {
  font-size: 48px;
  font-weight: 300;
  letter-spacing: 2px;
}
```

You should see the first stylings taking effect in your application when you start it again. Next, we will head over to the Item component. Some of its elements receive the `className` attribute too, however, we are also using a new styling technique here:

src/App.jsx

```jsx
const Item = ({ item, onRemoveItem }) => (
  <li className="item">
    <span style={{ width: '40%' }}>
      <a href={item.url}>{item.title}</a>
    </span>
    <span style={{ width: '30%' }}>{item.author}</span>
    <span style={{ width: '10%' }}>{item.num_comments}</span>
    <span style={{ width: '10%' }}>{item.points}</span>
    <span style={{ width: '10%' }}>
      <button
        type="button"
        onClick={() => onRemoveItem(item)}
        className="button button_small"
      >
        Dismiss
      </button>
    </span>
  </li>
);
```

As you can see, we can also use the `style` attribute for HTML elements. In JSX, style can be passed as an inline JavaScript object to these attributes. This way we can define dynamic style properties in JavaScript files rather than mostly static CSS files. This approach is called **inline style**, which is useful for quick prototyping and dynamic style definitions. Inline style should be used sparingly, however, since a separate style definition with a CSS file keeps the JSX more concise.

In your *src/App.css* file, define the new CSS classes. Basic CSS features are used here, because advanced CSS features (e.g. nesting) from CSS extensions (e.g. Sass) are not included in this example, as they are optional configurations[254]:

src/App.css

```css
.item {
  display: flex;
  align-items: center;
  padding-bottom: 5px;
}

.item > span {
  padding: 0 5px;
  white-space: nowrap;
  overflow: hidden;
  white-space: nowrap;
  text-overflow: ellipsis;
}

.item > span > a {
  color: inherit;
}
```

The button style from the previous component is still missing, so we'll define a base button style and two more specific button styles (small and large). One of the button specifications has been already used, the other will be used in the next steps:

---

[254]https://bit.ly/3E1a2bM

src/App.css

```css
.button {
  background: transparent;
  border: 1px solid #171212;
  padding: 5px;
  cursor: pointer;

  transition: all 0.1s ease-in;
}

.button:hover {
  background: #171212;
  color: #ffffff;
}

.button_small {
  padding: 5px;
}

.button_large {
  padding: 10px;
}
```

Apart from styling approaches in React, naming conventions (CSS guidelines[255]) are a whole other topic. The last CSS snippet followed BEM rules by defining modifications of a class with an underscore (_). Choose whatever naming convention suits you and your team. Without further ado, we will style the next React component:

src/App.jsx

```jsx
const SearchForm = ({ ... }) => (
  <form onSubmit={onSearchSubmit} className="search-form">
    <InputWithLabel ... >
      <strong>Search:</strong>
    </InputWithLabel>

    <button
      type="submit"
      disabled={!searchTerm}
      className="button button_large"
    >
      Submit
```

[255]https://mzl.la/3m5avnb

```
      </button>
    </form>
  );
```

We can also pass the `className` attribute as a prop to React components. For example, we can use this option to pass the SearchForm component a flexible style with a `className` prop from a range of predefined classes (e.g. `button_large` or `button_small`) from a CSS file. Lastly, style the InputWithLabel component:

src/App.jsx

```
const InputWithLabel = ({ ... }) => {
  ...

  return (
    <>
      <label htmlFor={id} className="label">
        {children}
      </label>
       
      <input
        ref={inputRef}
        id={id}
        type={type}
        value={value}
        onChange={onInputChange}
        className="input"
      />
    </>
  );
};
```

In your *src/App.css* file, add the remaining classes:

src/App.css

```
.search-form {
  padding: 10px 0 20px 0;
  display: flex;
  align-items: baseline;
}

.label {
  border-top: 1px solid #171212;
  border-left: 1px solid #171212;
  padding-left: 5px;
  font-size: 24px;
}

.input {
  border: none;
  border-bottom: 1px solid #171212;
  background-color: transparent;

  font-size: 24px;
}
```

For simplicity, we styled elements like label and input individually in the *src/App.css* file. However, in a real application, it may be better to define these elements once in the *src/index.css* file globally. As React components are split into multiple files, sharing style becomes a necessity. After all, this is the basic usage of CSS in React. Without CSS extensions like Sass (Syntactically Awesome Style Sheets), styling can become more burdensome, though, because features like CSS nesting are not available in native CSS.

Exercises:

- Compare your source code against the author's source code[256].
  - Recap all the source code changes from this section[257].
- Try to pass className prop from App to SearchForm component, either with the value button_small or button_large, and use this as className for the button element.
- Optional: Leave feedback for this section[258].

---

[256]https://bit.ly/4b3Lik9
[257]https://bit.ly/4b4wdiA
[258]https://forms.gle/RovYbjYF9McD1h6c7

CSS Modules in React

CSS Modules are an advanced **CSS-in-CSS** approach. The CSS file stays the same, where you could apply CSS extensions like Sass, but its use in React components changes. To enable CSS modules in Vite, rename the *src/App.css* file to *src/App.module.css*. This action is performed on the command line from your project's directory:

Command Line

```
mv src/App.css src/App.module.css
```

In the renamed *src/App.module.css*, start with the first CSS class definitions, as before:

src/App.module.css

```css
.container {
  height: 100vw;
  padding: 20px;

  background: #83a4d4; /* fallback for old browsers */
  background: linear-gradient(to left, #b6fbff, #83a4d4);

  color: #171212;
}

.headlinePrimary {
  font-size: 48px;
  font-weight: 300;
  letter-spacing: 2px;
}
```

Import the *src/App.module.css* file with a relative path again. This time, import it as a JavaScript object where the name of the object (here: styles) is up to you:

src/App.jsx

```jsx
import * as React from 'react';
import axios from 'axios';

import styles from './App.module.css';
```

Instead of defining the className as a string mapped to a CSS file, access the CSS class directly from the styles object, and assign it with a JavaScript in JSX expression to your elements.

src/App.jsx

```
const App = () => {
  ...

  return (
    <div className={styles.container}>
      <h1 className={styles.headlinePrimary}>My Hacker Stories</h1>

      <SearchForm
        searchTerm={searchTerm}
        onSearchInput={handleSearchInput}
        onSearchSubmit={handleSearchSubmit}
      />

      {stories.isError && <p>Something went wrong ...</p>}

      {stories.isLoading ? (
        <p>Loading ...</p>
      ) : (
        <List list={stories.data} onRemoveItem={handleRemoveStory} />
      )}
    </div>
  );
};
```

There are various ways to add multiple CSS classes via the styles object to the element's single className attribute. Here, we use JavaScript template literals:

src/App.jsx

```
const Item = ({ item, onRemoveItem }) => (
  <li className={styles.item}>
    <span style={{ width: '40%' }}>
      <a href={item.url}>{item.title}</a>
    </span>
    <span style={{ width: '30%' }}>{item.author}</span>
    <span style={{ width: '10%' }}>{item.num_comments}</span>
    <span style={{ width: '10%' }}>{item.points}</span>
    <span style={{ width: '10%' }}>
      <button
        type="button"
        onClick={() => onRemoveItem(item)}
        className={`${styles.button} ${styles.buttonSmall}`}
```

```
        >
          Dismiss
        </button>
      </span>
    </li>
);
```

We can also add inline styles as more dynamic styles in JSX again. It's also possible to add a CSS extension like Sass to enable advanced features like CSS nesting (see the previous section). We will stick to native CSS features though:

src/App.module.css

```css
.item {
  display: flex;
  align-items: center;
  padding-bottom: 5px;
}

.item > span {
  padding: 0 5px;
  white-space: nowrap;
  overflow: hidden;
  white-space: nowrap;
  text-overflow: ellipsis;
}

.item > span > a {
  color: inherit;
}
```

Then the button CSS classes in the *src/App.module.css* file:

src/App.module.css

```css
.button {
  background: transparent;
  border: 1px solid #171212;
  padding: 5px;
  cursor: pointer;

  transition: all 0.1s ease-in;
}
```

```
.button:hover {
  background: #171212;
  color: #ffffff;
}

.buttonSmall {
  padding: 5px;
}

.buttonLarge {
  padding: 10px;
}
```

There is a shift toward pseudo BEM naming conventions here, in contrast to button_small and button_large from the previous section. If the previous naming convention holds true, we can only access the style with styles['button_small'] which makes it more verbose because of JavaScript's limitation with object underscores. The same shortcomings would apply for classes defined with a dash (-). In contrast, now we can use styles.buttonSmall instead (see: Item component):

src/App.jsx

```
const SearchForm = ({ ... }) => (
  <form onSubmit={onSearchSubmit} className={styles.searchForm}>
    <InputWithLabel ... >
      <strong>Search:</strong>
    </InputWithLabel>

    <button
      type="submit"
      disabled={!searchTerm}
      className={`${styles.button} ${styles.buttonLarge}`}
    >
      Submit
    </button>
  </form>
);
```

The SearchForm component receives the styles as well. It has to use string interpolation for using two styles in one element via JavaScript's template literals. One alternative way is the clsx[259] library, which is installed via the command line as a project dependency:

---

[259]https://bit.ly/3DNEA3R

src/App.jsx

```
import clsx from 'clsx';

...

// somewhere in a className attribute
className={clsx(styles.button, styles.buttonLarge)}
```

The library offers conditional styling too; whereas the left-hand side of the object's property must be used as a computed property name[260] and is only applied if the right-hand side evaluates to true:

src/App.jsx

```
import clsx from 'clsx';

...

// somewhere in a className attribute
className={clsx(styles.button, { [styles.buttonLarge]: isLarge })}
```

Finally, continue with the InputWithLabel component:

src/App.jsx

```
const InputWithLabel = ({ ... }) => {
  ...

  return (
    <>
      <label htmlFor={id} className={styles.label}>
        {children}
      </label>
       
      <input
        ref={inputRef}
        id={id}
        type={type}
        value={value}
        onChange={onInputChange}
        className={styles.input}
      />
    </>
```

---

[260]https://mzl.la/2XuN651

```
  );
};
```

And finish up the remaining style in the *src/App.module.css* file:

src/App.module.css

```css
.searchForm {
  padding: 10px 0 20px 0;
  display: flex;
  align-items: baseline;
}

.label {
  border-top: 1px solid #171212;
  border-left: 1px solid #171212;
  padding-left: 5px;
  font-size: 24px;
}

.input {
  border: none;
  border-bottom: 1px solid #171212;
  background-color: transparent;

  font-size: 24px;
}
```

The same caution as the last section applies: some of these styles like input and label might be more efficient in a global *src/index.css* file without CSS modules.

Again, CSS Modules – like any other CSS-in-CSS approach – can use Sass for more advanced CSS features like nesting. The advantage of CSS modules is that we receive an error in JavaScript each time a style isn't defined. In the standard CSS approach, unmatched styles in JavaScript and CSS files might go unnoticed.

Exercises:

- Compare your source code against the author's source code[261].
  – Recap all the source code changes from this section[262].
- Optional: Leave feedback for this section[263].

---

[261]https://bit.ly/490UtQu
[262]https://bit.ly/3tYvKxt
[263]https://forms.gle/iuU7WaeJVwHN2pFCA

Styled Components in React

With the previous approaches from CSS-in-CSS, Styled Components is one of several approaches for **CSS-in-JS**. I picked Styled Components because it's the most popular. It comes as a JavaScript dependency, so we must install it on the command line:

Command Line

```
npm install styled-components
```

Then import it in your *src/App.jsx* file:

src/App.jsx

```
import * as React from 'react';
import axios from 'axios';
import styled from 'styled-components';
```

As the name suggests, CSS-in-JS happens in your JavaScript file. In your *src/App.jsx* file, define your first styled components:

src/App.jsx

```
const StyledContainer = styled.div`
  height: 100vw;
  padding: 20px;

  background: #83a4d4;
  background: linear-gradient(to left, #b6fbff, #83a4d4);

  color: #171212;
`;

const StyledHeadlinePrimary = styled.h1`
  font-size: 48px;
  font-weight: 300;
  letter-spacing: 2px;
`;
```

When using Styled Components, you are using the JavaScript template literals the same way as JavaScript functions. Everything between the backticks can be seen as an argument and the `styled` object gives you access to all the necessary HTML elements (e.g. div, h1) as functions. Once a function is called with the style, it returns a React component that can be used in your App component:

src/App.jsx

```
const App = () => {
  ...

  return (
    <StyledContainer>
      <StyledHeadlinePrimary>My Hacker Stories</StyledHeadlinePrimary>

      <SearchForm
        searchTerm={searchTerm}
        onSearchInput={handleSearchInput}
        onSearchSubmit={handleSearchSubmit}
      />

      {stories.isError && <p>Something went wrong ...</p>}

      {stories.isLoading ? (
        <p>Loading ...</p>
      ) : (
        <List list={stories.data} onRemoveItem={handleRemoveStory} />
      )}
    </StyledContainer>
  );
};
```

This kind of React component follows the same rules as a common React component. Everything passed between its element tags is passed automatically as React `children` prop. For the Item component, we are not using inline styles this time, but defining a dedicated styled component for it. `StyledColumn` receives its styles dynamically using a React prop:

src/App.jsx

```
const Item = ({ item, onRemoveItem }) => (
  <StyledItem>
    <StyledColumn width="40%">
      <a href={item.url}>{item.title}</a>
    </StyledColumn>
    <StyledColumn width="30%">{item.author}</StyledColumn>
    <StyledColumn width="10%">{item.num_comments}</StyledColumn>
    <StyledColumn width="10%">{item.points}</StyledColumn>
    <StyledColumn width="10%">
      <StyledButtonSmall
        type="button"
```

```
      onClick={() => onRemoveItem(item)}
    >
      Dismiss
    </StyledButtonSmall>
  </StyledColumn>
</StyledItem>
);
```

The flexible `width` prop is accessible in the styled component's template literal as an argument of an inline function. The return value from the function is applied there as a string. Since we can use immediate returns when omitting the arrow function's body, it becomes a concise inline function:

src/App.jsx

```
const StyledItem = styled.li`
  display: flex;
  align-items: center;
  padding-bottom: 5px;
`;

const StyledColumn = styled.span`
  padding: 0 5px;
  white-space: nowrap;
  overflow: hidden;
  white-space: nowrap;
  text-overflow: ellipsis;

  a {
    color: inherit;
  }

  width: ${(props) => props.width};
`;
```

Advanced features like CSS nesting are available in Styled Components by default. Nested elements are accessible and the current element can be selected with the & CSS operator:

src/App.jsx

```
const StyledButton = styled.button`
  background: transparent;
  border: 1px solid #171212;
  padding: 5px;
  cursor: pointer;

  transition: all 0.1s ease-in;

  &:hover {
    background: #171212;
    color: #ffffff;
  }
`;
```

You can also create specialized versions of styled components by passing another component to the library's function. The specialized button receives all the base styles from the previously defined StyledButton component:

src/App.jsx

```
const StyledButtonSmall = styled(StyledButton)`
  padding: 5px;
`;

const StyledButtonLarge = styled(StyledButton)`
  padding: 10px;
`;

const StyledSearchForm = styled.form`
  padding: 10px 0 20px 0;
  display: flex;
  align-items: baseline;
`;
```

When we use a styled component like StyledSearchForm, its underlying form element is used in the real HTML output. We can continue using the native HTML attributes (onSubmit, type, disabled) there:

src/App.jsx

```
const SearchForm = ({ ... }) => (
  <StyledSearchForm onSubmit={onSearchSubmit}>
    <InputWithLabel
      id="search"
      value={searchTerm}
      isFocused
      onInputChange={onSearchInput}
    >
      <strong>Search:</strong>
    </InputWithLabel>

    <StyledButtonLarge type="submit" disabled={!searchTerm}>
      Submit
    </StyledButtonLarge>
  </StyledSearchForm>
);
```

Finally, the InputWithLabel decorated with its yet undefined styled components:

src/App.jsx

```
const InputWithLabel = ({ ... }) => {
  ...

  return (
    <>
      <StyledLabel htmlFor={id}>{children}</StyledLabel>
       
      <StyledInput
        ref={inputRef}
        id={id}
        type={type}
        value={value}
        onChange={onInputChange}
      />
    </>
  );
};
```

And its matching styled components are defined in the same file:

src/App.jsx

```
const StyledLabel = styled.label`
  border-top: 1px solid #171212;
  border-left: 1px solid #171212;
  padding-left: 5px;
  font-size: 24px;
`;

const StyledInput = styled.input`
  border: none;
  border-bottom: 1px solid #171212;
  background-color: transparent;

  font-size: 24px;
`;
```

CSS-in-JS with styled components shifts the focus of defining styles to actual React components. Styled Components are styles defined as React components without the intermediate CSS file. If a styled component isn't used in a JavaScript, your IDE/editor will tell you. Styled Components are bundled next to other JavaScript assets in JavaScript files for a production-ready application. There are no extra CSS files, but only JavaScript when using the CSS-in-JS strategy. Both strategies, CSS-in-JS and CSS-in-CSS, and their approaches (e.g. Styled Components and CSS Modules) are popular among React developers. Use what suits you and your team best.

Exercises:

- Compare your source code against the author's source code[264].
  - Recap all the source code changes from this section[265].
- Read more about best practices for Styled Components in React[266].
- Usually there is no *src/index.css* file for global styles when using Styled Components. Find out how to use global styles when using Styled Components with the help of your favorite search engine.
- Optional: Leave feedback for this section[267].

---

[264]https://bit.ly/48UtG8s
[265]https://bit.ly/3SpLli3
[266]https://www.robinwieruch.de/styled-components/
[267]https://forms.gle/5vFxvg9hSNAna37S8

SVGs in React

To create a modern React application, we'll likely need to use SVGs. Instead of giving every button element text, for example, we might want to make it lightweight with an icon. In this section, we'll use a scalable vector graphic (SVG) as an icon in one of our React components.

Important: This section builds on the "CSS in React" we covered earlier which helps us giving the SVG icon a good look and feel right away. It's acceptable to use a different styling approach (e.g. CSS Modules, Styled Components), or no styling at all, though the SVG might look off without it.

Vite does not come with SVG support. In order to allow SVGs in Vite, we have to install one of Vite's plugins with the help of the command line:

Command Line

```
npm install vite-plugin-svgr --save-dev
```

Next the new plugin for SVGs can be used for Vite's configuration:

vite.config.js

```
import { defineConfig } from 'vite';
import react from '@vitejs/plugin-react';
import svgr from 'vite-plugin-svgr';

// https://vitejs.dev/config/
export default defineConfig({
  plugins: [react(), svgr()],
});
```

That's it for the general setup. We will use the following SVG[268] and create a new *src/check.svg* file:

src/check.svg

```
<?xml version="1.0" encoding="iso-8859-1"?>
<!-- Generator: Adobe Illustrator 18.0.0, SVG Export Plug-In . SVG Version: 6.00 Bui\
ld 0) -->
<!DOCTYPE svg PUBLIC "-//W3C//DTD SVG 1.1//EN" "http://www.w3.org/Graphics/SVG/1.1/D\
TD/svg11.dtd">
<svg version="1.1" id="Capa_1" xmlns="http://www.w3.org/2000/svg" xmlns:xlink="http:\
//www.w3.org/1999/xlink" x="0px" y="0px"
   viewBox="0 0 297 297" style="enable-background:new 0 0 297 297;" xml:space="prese\
rve">
  <g>
```

---

[268]https://bit.ly/3w4xNRz

```
    <path d="M113.636,272.638c-2.689,0-5.267-1.067-7.168-2.97L2.967,166.123c-3.956-3\
.957-3.956-10.371-0.001-14.329154.673-54.703
        c1.9-1.9,4.479-2.97,7.167-2.97c2.689,0,5.268,1.068,7.169,2.969141.661,41.676L2\
25.023,27.332c1.9-1.901,4.48-2.97,7.168-2.9710,0
        c2.688,0,5.268,1.068,7.167,2.97154.675,54.701c3.956,3.957,3.956,10.372,0,14.32\
8L120.803,269.668
        C118.903,271.57,116.325,272.638,113.636,272.638z M24.463,158.958189.173,89.209\
1158.9-158.971-40.346-40.364L120.803,160.264
        c-1.9,1.902-4.478,2.971-7.167,2.971c-2.688,0-5.267-1.068-7.168-2.971-41.66-41.\
674L24.463,158.958z"/>
    </g>
</svg>
```

Now we can import SVGs (similar to CSS) as React components right away. In *src/App.jsx*, use the following syntax for importing the SVG:

src/App.jsx

```
import * as React from 'react';
import axios from 'axios';

import './App.css';

import { ReactComponent as Check } from './check.svg';
```

Here we are importing an SVG to be used as icon. However, this works for many different uses cases such as logos and backgrounds. Now, instead of the button "Dismiss" text, pass the SVG component with a height and width attribute:

src/App.jsx

```
const Item = ({ item, onRemoveItem }) => (
  <li className="item">
    <span style={{ width: '40%' }}>
      <a href={item.url}>{item.title}</a>
    </span>
    <span style={{ width: '30%' }}>{item.author}</span>
    <span style={{ width: '10%' }}>{item.num_comments}</span>
    <span style={{ width: '10%' }}>{item.points}</span>
    <span style={{ width: '10%' }}>
      <button
        type="button"
        onClick={() => onRemoveItem(item)}
        className="button button_small"
```

```
    >
      <Check height="18px" width="18px" />
    </button>
  </span>
  </li>
);
```

Regardless of the styling approach you are using, you can give your SVG icon in the button a hover effect too, because right now it doesn't look right for the hover state. In the basic CSS approach, it would look like the following in the *src/App.css* file:

src/**App.css**

```
.button:hover > svg > g {
  fill: #ffffff;
  stroke: #ffffff;
}
```

The Vite plugin makes using SVGs straightforward, with not much extra configuration needed. This is different if you create a React project from scratch with build tools like Webpack, because you have to take care of it yourself. Anyway, SVGs make your application more approachable, so use them whenever it suits you.

Exercises:

- Compare your source code against the author's source code[269].
  - Recap all the source code changes from this section[270].
- Integrate the third-party library react-icons[271] into your application and use its SVG symbols by importing them as React components right away.
- Optional: Leave feedback for this section[272].

---

[269]https://bit.ly/4b1ZPge
[270]https://bit.ly/3U6XJpr
[271]https://bit.ly/3nayoJ7
[272]https://forms.gle/3yGgMDR2VQ5WksSXA

React Maintenance

Once a React application grows, maintenance becomes a priority. To prepare for this eventuality, we'll cover performance optimization, type safety, testing, and project structure. Each of these topics will strengthen your app to take on more functionality without losing quality.

Performance optimization prevents applications from slowing down by assuring efficient use of available resource. Typed programming languages like TypeScript detect bugs earlier in the feedback loop. Testing gives us more explicit feedback than typed programming, and provides a way to understand which actions can break the application. Lastly, a project structure supports the organized management of assets into folders and files, which is especially useful in scenarios where team members work in different domains.

Performance in React (Advanced)

This section is just here for the sake of learning about performance improvements in React. We wouldn't need optimizations in most React applications, as React is fast out of the box. While more sophisticated tools exist for performance measurements in JavaScript and React, we will stick to a simple `console.log()` and our browser's developer tools for the logging output.

Strict Mode

Before we can learn about performance in React, we will briefly look at React's Strict Mode which gets enabled in the *src/main.jsx* file:

src/main.jsx

```
ReactDOM.createRoot(document.getElementById('root')).render(
  <React.StrictMode>
    <App />
  </React.StrictMode>
);
```

React's Strict Mode[273] is a helper component which notifies developers in the case of something being wrong in our implementation. For example, using a deprecated[274] React API (e.g. using a legacy React hook) would give us a warning in the browser's developer tools. However, it also ensures that state and side-effects are implemented well by a developer. Let's experience what this means in our code.

The App component fetches initially data from a remote API which gets displayed as a list. We are using React's useEffect hook for initializing the data fetching. Now I encourage you to add a `console.log()` which logs whenever this hook runs:

src/main.jsx

```
const App = () => {
  ...

  React.useEffect(() => {
    console.log('How many times do I log?');
    handleFetchStories();
  }, [handleFetchStories]);

  ...
};
```

---
[273]https://bit.ly/48TUA0k
[274]https://bit.ly/3R8ycam

Many would expect seeing the logging only once in the browser's developer tools, because this side-effect should only run once (or if the `handleFetchStories` function changes). However, you will see the logging twice for the App component's initial render. To be honest, this is a highly unexpected behavior (even for seasoned React developers), which makes it difficult to understand for React beginners. However, the React core team decided that this behavior is needed for surfacing bugs related to misused side-effects in the application.

So React's Strict Mode runs React's useEffect Hooks twice for the initial render. Because this results in fetching the *same* data twice, this is not a problem for us. The operation is called idempotent, which means that the result of a successfully performed request is independent of the number of times it is executed. After all, it's *only* a performance problem, because there are two network requests, but it doesn't result in a buggy behavior of the application. In addition to all of this uncertainty, the Strict Mode is only applied for the development environment, so whenever this application gets build for production, the Strict Mode gets removed automatically.

Both of these behaviors, running React's useEffect Hook twice for the initial render and having different outcomes between development and production, surface many warranted discussions around React's Strict Mode.

For the following performance sections, I encourage you to disable the Strict Mode by simply removing it. This way, we can follow the logging that would happen for this application once it is build for a production environment:

src/main.jsx

```
ReactDOM.createRoot(document.getElementById('root')).render(
  <App />
);
```

However, at the end of the performance sections, I encourage you to add the Strict Mode back again, because it is there to help you after all.

Don't run on first render

Previously, we have covered React's useEffect Hook, which is used for side-effects. It runs the first time a component renders (mounting), and then every re-render (updating). By passing an empty dependency array to it as a second argument, we can tell the hook to run on the first render only. Out of the box, there is no way to tell the hook to run only on every re-render (update) and not on the first render (mount). For example, examine our custom hook for state management with React's useState Hook and its semi-persistent state with local storage using React's useEffect Hook:

src/App.jsx

```
const useStorageState = (key, initialState) => {
  const [value, setValue] = React.useState(
    localStorage.getItem(key) || initialState
  );

  React.useEffect(() => {
    console.log('A');
    localStorage.setItem(key, value);
  }, [value, key]);

  return [value, setValue];
};
```

With a closer look at the developer's tools, we can see the log for the first time when the component renders using this custom hook. It doesn't make sense to run the side-effect for the initial rendering of the component though, because there is nothing to store in the local storage except the initial value. It's a redundant function invocation, and should only run for every update (re-rendering) of the component.

As mentioned, there is no React Hook that runs on every re-render, and there is no way to tell the useEffect hook in a React idiomatic way to call its function only on every re-render. However, by using React's useRef Hook which keeps its ref.current property intact over re-renders, we can keep a *made up state* (without re-rendering the component on state updates) with an instance variable of our component's lifecycle:

src/App.jsx

```
const useStorageState = (key, initialState) => {
  const isMounted = React.useRef(false);

  const [value, setValue] = React.useState(
    localStorage.getItem(key) || initialState
  );

  React.useEffect(() => {
    if (!isMounted.current) {
      isMounted.current = true;
    } else {
      console.log('A');
      localStorage.setItem(key, value);
    }
  }, [value, key]);
```

```
    return [value, setValue];
};
```

We are exploiting the `ref` and its mutable `current` property for imperative state management that doesn't trigger a re-render. Once the hook is called from its component for the first time (component render), the ref's `current` property is initialized with a `false` boolean called `isMounted`. As a result, the side-effect function in `useEffect` isn't called; only the boolean flag for `isMounted` is toggled to `true` in the side-effect. Whenever the hook runs again (component re-render), the boolean flag is evaluated in the side-effect. Since it's `true`, the side-effect function runs. Over the lifetime of the component, the `isMounted` boolean will remain `true`. It was there to avoid calling the side-effect function for the first time render that uses our custom hook.

The above was only about preventing the invocation of one simple function for a component rendering for the first time. But imagine you have an expensive computation in your side-effect, or the custom hook is used frequently in the application. It's more practical to deploy this technique to avoid unnecessary function invocations.

Exercises:

- Read more about running useEffect only on update[275].
- Read more about running useEffect only once[276].

Don't re-render if not needed

Earlier, we have explored React's re-rendering mechanism. We'll repeat this exercise for the App and List components. For both components, add a logging statement:

src/App.jsx

```
const App = () => {
  ...

  console.log('B:App');

  return ( ... );
};

const List = ({ list, onRemoveItem }) =>
  console.log('B:List') || (
    <ul>
      {list.map((item) => (
```

---

[275]https://www.robinwieruch.de/react-useeffect-only-on-update/
[276]https://www.robinwieruch.de/react-useeffect-only-once/

```
    <Item
      key={item.objectID}
      item={item}
      onRemoveItem={onRemoveItem}
    />
  ))}
  </ul>
);
```

Because the List component has no function body, and developers are lazy folks who don't want to refactor the component for a simple logging statement, the List component uses the || operator instead. This is a neat trick for adding a logging statement to a function component without a function body. Since the console.log() on the left-hand side of the operator always evaluates to false, the right-hand side of the operator gets always executed.

Code Playground

```
function getTheTruth() {
  if (console.log('B:List')) {
    return true;
  } else {
    return false;
  }
}

console.log(getTheTruth());
// B:List
// false
```

Let's focus on the actual logging in the browser's developer tools when refreshing the page. You should see a similar output. First, the App component renders, followed by its child components (e.g. List component).

Visualization

```
B:App
B:List
B:App
B:App
B:List
```

*Again: If you are seeing more than these loggings, check whether your *src/main.jsx* file uses* <React.StrictMode> *as a wrapper for your App component. If it's the case, remove the Strict Mode and check your logging again. Explanation: In development mode, React's Strict Mode renders a* component twice to detect problems with your implementation in order to warn you about these. This Strict Mode is automatically excluded for applications in production. However, if you don't want to be confused by the multiple renders, remove Strict Mode from the *src/main.jsx* file.*

Since a side-effect triggers data fetching after the first render, only the App component renders, because the List component is replaced by a loading indicator in a conditional rendering. Once the data arrives, both components render again.

Visualization

```
// initial render
B:App
B:List

// data fetching with loading instead of List component
B:App

// re-rendering with data
B:App
B:List
```

So far, this behavior is acceptable, since everything renders on time. Now we'll take this experiment a step further, by typing into the SearchForm component's input field. You should see the changes with every character entered into the element:

Visualization

```
B:App
B:List
```

What's striking is that the List component shouldn't re-render, but it does. The search feature isn't executed via its button, so the list passed to the List component via the App component remains the same for every keystroke. This is React's default behavior, re-rendering everything below a component (here: the App component) with a state change, which surprises many people. In other words, if a parent component re-renders, its descendent components re-render as well. React does this by default, because preventing a re-render of child components could lead to bugs. Because the re-rendering mechanism of React is often fast enough by default, the automatic re-rendering of descendent components is encouraged by React.

Sometimes we want to prevent re-rendering, however. For example, huge data sets displayed in a table (e.g. List component) shouldn't re-render if they are not affected by an update (e.g. Search component). It's more efficient to perform an equality check if something changed for the component. Therefore, we can use React's memo API to make this equality check for the props:

src/App.jsx

```
const List = React.memo(
  ({ list, onRemoveItem }) =>
    console.log('B:List') || (
      <ul>
        {list.map((item) => (
          <Item
            key={item.objectID}
            item={item}
            onRemoveItem={onRemoveItem}
          />
        ))}
      </ul>
    )
);
```

React's memo API checks whether the props of a component have changed. If not, it does not re-render even though its parent component re-rendered. However, the output stays the same when typing into the SearchForm's input field:

Visualization

```
B:App
B:List
```

The list passed to the List component is the same, but the onRemoveItem callback handler isn't. If the App component re-renders, it always creates a new version of this callback handler as a new function. Earlier, we used React's useCallback Hook to prevent this behavior, by creating a function only on the initial render (or if one of its dependencies has changed):

src/App.jsx

```
const App = () => {
  ...

  const handleRemoveStory = React.useCallback((item) => {
    dispatchStories({
      type: 'REMOVE_STORY',
      payload: item,
    });
  }, []);

  ...
```

```
    console.log('B:App');

    return (... );
};
```

Since the callback handler gets the item passed as an argument in its function signature, it doesn't have any dependencies and is declared only once when the App component initially renders. None of the props passed to the List component should change now. Try it with the combination of React memo and useCallback, to search via the SearchForm's input field. The "B:List" logging disappears, and only the App component re-renders with its "B:App" logging.

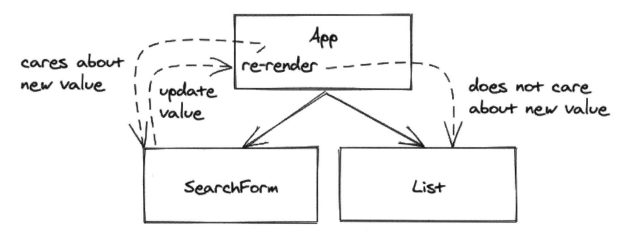

While all props passed to a component stay the same, the component renders again if its parent component is forced to re-render. That's React's default behavior, which works most of the time because the re-rendering mechanism is pretty fast. However, if re-rendering decreases the performance of a React application, React's memo API helps prevent re-rendering. As we have seen, sometimes memo alone doesn't help, though. Callback handlers are re-defined each time in the parent component and passed as *changed* props to the component, which causes another re-render. In that case, useCallback is used for making the callback handler only change when its dependencies change.

Exercises:

- Read more about React's memo API[277].
- Read more about React's useCallback Hook[278].

Don't rerun expensive computations

Sometimes we'll have performance-intensive computations in our React components – between a component's function signature and return block – which run on every render. For this scenario, we

---

[277]https://www.robinwieruch.de/react-memo/
[278]https://www.robinwieruch.de/react-usecallback-hook/

must create a use case in our current application first:

src/App.jsx

```
const getSumComments = (stories) => {
  console.log('C');

  return stories.data.reduce(
    (result, value) => result + value.num_comments,
    0
  );
};

const App = () => {
  ...

  const sumComments = getSumComments(stories);

  return (
    <div>
      <h1>My Hacker Stories with {sumComments} comments.</h1>

      ...
    </div>
  );
};
```

If all arguments are passed to a function, it's acceptable to have it outside the component, because it does not have any further dependency needed from within the component. This prevents creating the function on every render, so the useCallback hook becomes unnecessary. However, the function still computes the value of summed comments on every render, which becomes a problem for more expensive computations.

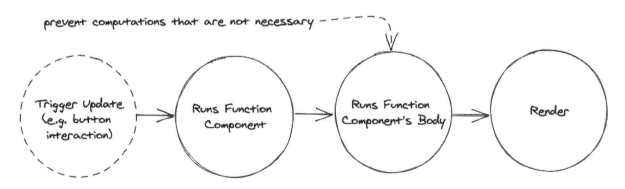

Each time text is typed in the input field of the SearchForm component, this computation runs again with an output of "C". This may be fine for a non-heavy computation like this one, but imagine this computation would take more than 500ms. It would give the re-rendering a delay, because everything in the component has to wait for this computation. We can tell React to only run a function if one of its dependencies has changed. If no dependency changed, the result of the function stays the same. React's useMemo Hook helps us here:

src/App.jsx

```
const App = () => {

  ...

  const sumComments = React.useMemo(
    () => getSumComments(stories),
    [stories]
  );

  return ( ... );
};
```

For every time someone types in the SearchForm, the computation shouldn't run again. It only runs if the dependency array, here stories, has changed. After all, this should only be used for cost expensive computations which could lead to a delay of a (re-)rendering of a component.

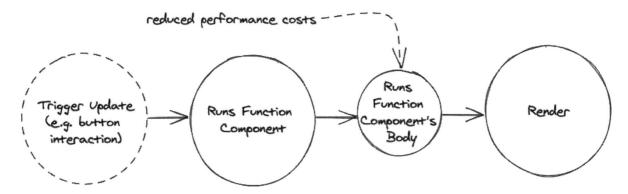

Now, after we went through these scenarios for useMemo, useCallback, and memo, remember that these shouldn't necessarily be used by default. Apply these performance optimizations only if you run into performance bottlenecks. Most of the time this shouldn't happen, because React's rendering mechanism is pretty efficient by default. Sometimes the check for utilities like memo can be more expensive than the re-rendering itself.

Exercises:

- Compare your source code against the author's source code[279].

---
[279]https://bit.ly/3OaOkcy

- – Recap all the source code changes from this section[280].
- Read more about React's useMemo Hook[281].
- Download *React Developer Tools* as an extension for your browser. Open it for your application in the browser via the browser's developer tools and try its various features. For example, you can use it to visualize React's component tree and its updating components.
- Does the SearchForm re-render when removing an item from the List with the "Dismiss"-button? If it's the case, apply performance optimization techniques (using `useCallback` and `memo`) to prevent re-rendering.
- Does each Item re-render when removing an item from the List with the "Dismiss"-button? If it's the case, apply performance optimization techniques to prevent re-rendering.
- Remove all performance optimizations to keep the application simple. Our current application doesn't suffer from any performance bottlenecks. Try to avoid premature optimzations[282]. Use this section and its further reading material as a reference, in case you run into performance problems.
- Optional: Leave feedback for this section[283].

---

[280]https://bit.ly/3U7ckBs
[281]https://www.robinwieruch.de/react-usememo-hook/
[282]https://bit.ly/3AYktL8
[283]https://forms.gle/FwNrJSdLikquVzsB6

TypeScript in React

TypeScript for JavaScript and React has many benefits for developing robust applications. Instead of getting type errors on runtime on the command line or browser, TypeScript integration presents them during compile time inside the IDE. It shortens the feedback loop for a developer, while it improves the developer experience. In addition, the code becomes more self-documenting and readable, because every variable is defined with a type. Also moving code blocks or performing a larger refactoring of a codebase becomes much more efficient. Statically typed languages like TypeScript are trending because of their benefits over dynamically typed languages like JavaScript. It's useful to learn more about TypeScript[284] whenever possible.

TypeScript Setup

To use TypeScript in React (with Vite), install TypeScript and its dependencies into your application using the command line:

Command Line

```
npm install typescript @types/react @types/react-dom --save-dev
npm install @typescript-eslint/eslint-plugin --save-dev
npm install @typescript-eslint/parser --save-dev
```

Add two TypeScript configuration files; one for the browser environment and one for the Node environment:

Command Line

```
touch tsconfig.json tsconfig.node.json
```

In the TypeScript file for the browser environment include the following configuration:

tsconfig.json

```
{
  "compilerOptions": {
    "target": "ES2020",
    "useDefineForClassFields": true,
    "lib": ["ES2020", "DOM", "DOM.Iterable"],
    "module": "ESNext",
    "skipLibCheck": true,

    /* Bundler mode */
    "moduleResolution": "bundler",
```

---
[284]https://bit.ly/3G0l3vL

```
    "allowImportingTsExtensions": true,
    "resolveJsonModule": true,
    "isolatedModules": true,
    "noEmit": true,
    "jsx": "react-jsx",

    /* Linting */
    "strict": true,
    "noUnusedLocals": true,
    "noUnusedParameters": true,
    "noFallthroughCasesInSwitch": true
  },
  "include": ["src"],
  "references": [{ "path": "./tsconfig.node.json" }]
}
```

Then In the TypeScript file for the Node environment include some more configuration:

tsconfig.node.json

```
{
  "compilerOptions": {
    "composite": true,
    "skipLibCheck": true,
    "module": "ESNext",
    "moduleResolution": "bundler",
    "allowSyntheticDefaultImports": true
  },
  "include": ["vite.config.ts"]
}
```

If you have a ESLint configuration, you need to adapt it to TypeScript too:

.eslintrc.cjs

```
module.exports = {
  root: true,
  env: { browser: true, es2020: true },
  extends: [
    'eslint:recommended',
    'plugin:@typescript-eslint/recommended',
    'plugin:react-hooks/recommended',
  ],
  ignorePatterns: ['dist', '.eslintrc.cjs'],
```

```
  parser: '@typescript-eslint/parser',
  plugins: ['react-refresh'],
  rules: {
    'react-refresh/only-export-components': [
      'warn',
      { allowConstantExport: true },
    ],
  },
};
```

Next, rename all JavaScript files (*.jsx*) to TypeScript files (*.tsx*).

Command Line

```
mv src/main.jsx src/main.tsx
mv src/App.jsx src/App.tsx
```

And in your *index.html* file, reference the new TypeScript file instead of a JavaScript file:

index.html

```html
<!DOCTYPE html>
<html lang="en">
  <head>
    <meta charset="UTF-8" />
    <link rel="icon" type="image/svg+xml" href="/vite.svg" />
    <meta name="viewport" content="width=device-width, initial-scale=1.0" />
    <title>Vite + React</title>
  </head>
  <body>
    <div id="root"></div>
    <script type="module" src="/src/main.tsx"></script>
  </body>
</html>
```

You may also need a new vite-env.d.ts file in your project's root with the following content:

index.html

```
/// <reference types="vite/client" />
```

Restart your development server on the command line. You may encounter compile errors in the browser and editor/IDE. If you don't see any errors in your editor/IDE when opening the renamed TypeScript files (e.g. *src/App.tsx*), try installing a TypeScript plugin for your editor or a TypeScript extension for your IDE. Usually you should see red lines under all the values where TypeScript definitions are missing.

Type Safety for Functions and Components

The application should still start, however, we are missing type definitions in the *src/main.tsx* and *src/App.tsx* files. Let's start with the former one, because this is only a little change:

src/main.tsx

```
import React from 'react';
import ReactDOM from 'react-dom/client';
import App from './App';

ReactDOM.createRoot(document.getElementById('root')!).render(
  <React.StrictMode>
    <App />
  </React.StrictMode>
);
```

Without this change, TypeScript should output us the following error: *Argument of type 'HTMLElement | null' is not assignable to parameter of type 'Element | DocumentFragment'.*. It can be translated as: "The returned HTML element from getElementById() could be null if there is no such HTML element, but createRoot() expects it to be an Element." Because we know for sure that there is a HTML element with this specific identifier in the *index.html* file, we are replying TypeScript with "I know better" by using a so called type assertion (here: as keyword) in TypeScript.

Next, we'll add type safety[285] for the entire *src/App.tsx* file. When looking at a custom React hook plainly from a programming language perspective, it is just another function. In TypeScript a function's input (and optionally output) has to be type safe though. Let's start by making our useStorageState() hook type safe where we are telling the function to expect two arguments as string primitives:

src/App.tsx

```
const useStorageState = (
  key: string,
  initialState: string
) => {
  const [value, setValue] = React.useState(
    localStorage.getItem(key) || initialState
  );

  React.useEffect(() => {
    localStorage.setItem(key, value);
  }, [value, key]);
```

---
[285]https://bit.ly/3jhm6xi

```
  return [value, setValue];
};
```

Also, we can tell the function to return an array ([]) with a first value (current state) of type `string` and a second value (state updater function) that takes a new value (new state) of type `string` to return nothing (`void`):

src/App.tsx

```
const useStorageState = (
  key: string,
  initialState: string
): [string, (newValue: string) => void] => {
  const [value, setValue] = React.useState(
    localStorage.getItem(key) || initialState
  );

  React.useEffect(() => {
    localStorage.setItem(key, value);
  }, [value, key]);

  return [value, setValue];
};
```

Since TypeScript could already infer this type from React's useState Hook, we could simply remove the return type again. However, we need to declare the returned array as TypeScript `const`, because otherwise the order of the entries in the array would not be known to other parts of the application:

src/App.tsx

```
const useStorageState = (key: string, initialState: string) => {
  const [value, setValue] = React.useState(
    localStorage.getItem(key) || initialState
  );

  React.useEffect(() => {
    localStorage.setItem(key, value);
  }, [value, key]);

  return [value, setValue] as const;
};
```

Related to React though, considering the previous type safety improvements for the custom hook, we hadn't to add types to the internal React hooks in the function's body. That's because **type inference** works most of the time for React hooks out of the box. If the *initial state* of a React useState Hook is a JavaScript string primitive, then the returned *current state* will be inferred as a string and the returned *state updater function* will only take a string as an argument and return nothing:

Code Playground

```
const [value, setValue] = React.useState('React');

// value is inferred to be a string
// setValue only takes a string as argument
```

However, if the *initial state* would be null initially, we would have to tell TypeScript all of React's useState Hook potential types (here with a so called union type in TypeScript where | makes a union of two or more types). A TypeScript generic[286] is used to tell the function (here: a React hook) about it:

Code Playground

```
const [value, setValue] = React.useState<string | null>(null);

// value has to be either a string or null
// setValue only takes a string or null as argument
```

If adding type safety becomes an aftermath for a React application and its components, like in our case, there are multiple ways on how to approach it. We will start with the props and state for the leaf components of our application. For example, the Item component receives a story (here: item) and a callback handler function (here: onRemoveItem). Starting out very verbose, we could add the inlined types for both function arguments as we did before:

src/App.tsx

```
const Item = ({
  item,
  onRemoveItem,
}: {
  item: {
    objectID: string;
    url: string;
    title: string;
    author: string;
    num_comments: number;
    points: number;
  };
  onRemoveItem: (item: {
    objectID: string;
    url: string;
```

---

[286]https://www.robinwieruch.de/typescript-generics/

```
    title: string;
    author: string;
    num_comments: number;
    points: number;
  }) => void;
}) => (
  <li>
    ...
  </li>
);
```

There are two problems: the code is verbose, and it has duplicates (see: item). Let's get rid of both problems by defining a custom Story type outside the component, at the top of *src/App.jsx*:

src/App.tsx

```
type Story = {
  objectID: string;
  url: string;
  title: string;
  author: string;
  num_comments: number;
  points: number;
};

...

const Item = ({
  item,
  onRemoveItem,
}: {
  item: Story;
  onRemoveItem: (item: Story) => void;
}) => (
  <li>
    ...
  </li>
);
```

The item is of type Story and the onRemoveItem function takes an item of type Story as an argument and returns nothing. Next, clean up the code by defining the props of the Item component as type outside of it:

src/App.tsx

```
type ItemProps = {
  item: Story;
  onRemoveItem: (item: Story) => void;
};

const Item = ({ item, onRemoveItem }: ItemProps) => (
  <li>
    ...
  </li>
);
```

From here, we can navigate up the component tree into the List component and apply the same type definitions for the props. First try it yourself and then check out the following implementation:

src/App.tsx

```
type ListProps = {
  list: Story[];
  onRemoveItem: (item: Story) => void;
};

const List = ({ list, onRemoveItem }: ListProps) => (
  <ul>
    ...
  </ul>
);
```

The onRemoveItem function is typed twice for the ItemProps and ListProps now. To be more accurate, you *could* extract this to a standalone defined OnRemoveItem TypeScript type and reuse it for both onRemoveItem prop type definitions. Note, however, that development becomes increasingly difficult as components are split up into different files. That's why we will keep the duplication here.

Next we can repurpose the Story type for other components. For instance, add the Story type to the callback handler in the App component:

src/App.tsx

```
const App = () => {

  ...

  const handleRemoveStory = (item: Story) => {
    dispatchStories({
      type: 'REMOVE_STORY',
      payload: item,
    });
  };


  ...
};
```

The reducer function manages the Story type as well, without really touching it due to state and action types. As the application's developer, we know both objects and their shapes that are passed to this reducer function:

src/App.tsx

```
type StoriesState = {
  data: Story[];
  isLoading: boolean;
  isError: boolean;
};

type StoriesAction = {
  type: string;
  payload: any;
};

const storiesReducer = (
  state: StoriesState,
  action: StoriesAction
) => {
  ...
};
```

The Action type with its string and any (TypeScript **wildcard**) type definitions are still too broad; and we gain no real type safety through it, because actions are not distinguishable. We can do better by specifying each action as a TypeScript type and using a union type (here: StoriesAction) for the final type safety:

src/App.tsx

```
type StoriesFetchInitAction = {
  type: 'STORIES_FETCH_INIT';
}

type StoriesFetchSuccessAction = {
  type: 'STORIES_FETCH_SUCCESS';
  payload: Story[];
}

type StoriesFetchFailureAction = {
  type: 'STORIES_FETCH_FAILURE';
}

type StoriesRemoveAction = {
  type: 'REMOVE_STORY';
  payload: Story;
}

type StoriesAction =
  StoriesFetchInitAction
  | StoriesFetchSuccessAction
  | StoriesFetchFailureAction
  | StoriesRemoveAction;

const storiesReducer = (
  state: StoriesState,
  action: StoriesAction
) => {
  ...
};
```

The reducer's current state, action, and returned state (inferred) are type safe now. For example, if you would dispatch an action to the reducer with an action type that's not defined, you would get an error from TypeScript. Or if you would pass something else than a story to the action which removes a story, you would get a type error as well. Now let's shift our focus to the SearchForm component, which has callback handlers with events:

src/App.tsx

```
type SearchFormProps = {
  searchTerm: string;
  onSearchInput: (event: React.ChangeEvent<HTMLInputElement>) => void;
  onSearchSubmit: (event: React.FormEvent<HTMLFormElement>) => void;
};

const SearchForm = ({
  searchTerm,
  onSearchInput,
  onSearchSubmit,
}: SearchFormProps) => (
  ...
);
```

Often using React.SyntheticEvent instead of React.ChangeEvent or React.FormEvent is usually sufficient. However, most often your applications requires a more specific type. Next, going up to the App component again, we apply the same type for the callback handler there:

src/App.tsx

```
const App = () => {
  ...

  const handleSearchInput = (
    event: React.ChangeEvent<HTMLInputElement>
  ) => {
    setSearchTerm(event.target.value);
  };

  const handleSearchSubmit = (
    event: React.FormEvent<HTMLFormElement>
  ) => {
    setUrl(`${API_ENDPOINT}${searchTerm}`);

    event.preventDefault();
  };

  ...
};
```

All that's left is the InputWithLabel component. Before handling this component's props, let's take a look at the ref from React's useRef Hook. Unfortunately, the return value isn't inferred:

src/App.tsx

```
const InputWithLabel = ({ ... }) => {
  const inputRef = React.useRef<HTMLInputElement>(null);

  React.useEffect(() => {
    if (isFocused && inputRef.current) {
      inputRef.current.focus();
    }
  }, [isFocused]);
```

We made the returned `ref` type safe and typed it as read-only, because we only execute the `focus` method on it (read). React takes over for us there, setting the DOM element to the `current` property.

Lastly, we will apply type safety checks for the InputWithLabel component's props. Note the `children` prop with its React specific type and the **optional types** are signaled with a question mark:

src/App.tsx

```
type InputWithLabelProps = {
  id: string;
  value: string;
  type?: string;
  onInputChange: (event: React.ChangeEvent<HTMLInputElement>) => void;
  isFocused?: boolean;
  children: React.ReactNode;
};

const InputWithLabel = ({
  id,
  value,
  type = 'text',
  onInputChange,
  isFocused,
  children,
}: InputWithLabelProps) => {
  ...
};
```

Both the `type` and `isFocused` properties are optional. Using TypeScript, you can tell the compiler that these don't need to be passed to the component as props. The `children` prop has a lot of TypeScript type definitions that could be applicable to this concept, the most universal of which is `React.ReactNode` from the React library.

Our entire React application is finally typed by TypeScript, making it easy to spot type errors on compile time. When adding TypeScript to your React application, start by adding type definitions to your function's arguments. These functions can be vanilla JavaScript functions, custom React hooks, or React function components. Only when using React is it important to know specific types for form elements, events, and JSX.

Exercises:

- Compare your source code against the author's source code[287].
  - Recap all the source code changes from this section[288].
- Dig into the React + TypeScript Cheatsheet[289], because most common use cases we faced in this section are covered there as well. There is no need to know everything from the top of your head.
- While you continue with the learning experience in the following sections, remove or keep your types with TypeScript. If you do the latter, add new types whenever you get a compile error.
- Optional: Leave feedback for this section[290].

---

[287]https://bit.ly/3S3yfGW
[288]https://bit.ly/48WSexM
[289]https://bit.ly/3phdf2H
[290]https://forms.gle/Pyw2oUjXV85hwk2t6

Testing in React

Testing source code is an essential part of programming and should be seen as a mandatory exercise for serious developers. The goal is to verify our source code's quality and functionality before using it in production. The testing pyramid[291] will serve as our guide.

The testing pyramid includes end-to-end tests, integration tests, and unit tests. Unit tests are for small, isolated blocks of code, such as a single function or component. Integration tests help us figure out how well these blocks of code work together. And end-to-end tests simulate a real-life scenario, like a user logging into a web application. While unit tests are quick and easy to write and maintain; end-to-end tests are the opposite.

Many unit tests are required to cover all the functions and components in a working application, after which several integration tests make sure that the most important units work together. The final touch give a few end-to-end tests to simulate critical user scenarios. In this section, we will cover **unit and integration tests**, in addition to a useful component-specific testing technique called **snapshot tests**. **E2E tests** will be part of the exercise.

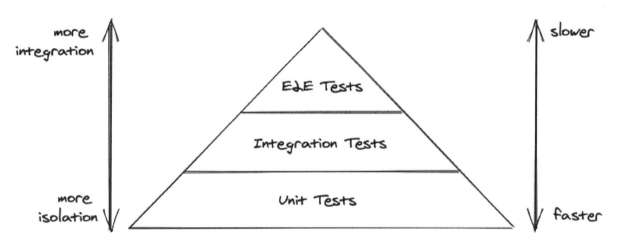

Choosing a testing library can be a challenge for React beginners, as there are many options. To keep things simple, we'll employ the most popular tools: Vitest[292] and React Testing Library[293] (RTL). Vitest is a full-blown testing framework with test runners, test suites, test cases, and assertions. RTL is used for rendering React components, triggering events like mouse clicks, and selecting HTML elements from the DOM to perform assertions. We'll explore both tools step-by-step, from setup to unit testing to integration testing.

Before we can write our first test, we have to install Vitest and set it up. Start by typing the following instruction on the command line:

---

[291]https://bit.ly/3BYEra1
[292]https://vitest.dev/
[293]https://testing-library.com

Command Line

```
npm install vitest --save-dev
```

Then in your package.json file, add another script which will run the tests eventually:

package.json

```
"dev": "vite",
"build": "vite build",
"test": "vitest",
"test": "vitest",
"lint": "eslint . --ext js,jsx --report-unused-disable-directives --max-warnings 0",
"preview": "vite preview"
```

Last, create a new file for testing functions and components:

Command Line

```
touch src/App.test.jsx
```

From there we will start writing tests for features that come from the *src/App.jsx* file next to it.

Test Suites, Test Cases, and Assertions

Test suites and test cases are commonly used in JavaScript and many other programming languages. A test suite groups the individual test cases into one larger subject. Let's see how this looks with Vitest in our *src/App.test.jsx* file:

src/App.test.jsx

```
import { describe, it, expect } from 'vitest';

describe('something truthy and falsy', () => {
  it('true to be true', () => {
    expect(true).toBe(true);
  });

  it('false to be false', () => {
    expect(false).toBe(false);
  });
});
```

The "describe" block is our *test suite*, and the "it" blocks are our *test cases*. Note that test cases can be used without test suites:

src/App.test.jsx

```
import { it, expect } from 'vitest';

it('true to be true', () => {
  expect(true).toBe(true);
});

it('false to be false', () => {
  expect(false).toBe(false);
});
```

Large subjects like functions or components often require multiple test cases, so it makes sense to use them with test suites:

Code Playground

```
describe('App component', () => {
  it('removes an item when clicking the Dismiss button', () => {

  });

  it('requests some initial stories from an API', () => {

  });
});
```

Finally you can run tests using the test script from your *package.json* on the command line with npm run test to produce the following output:

Command Line

```
 ✓ src/App.test.jsx (2)
   ✓ something truthy and falsy (2)
     ✓ true to be true
     ✓ false to be false

 Test Files  1 passed (1)
      Tests  2 passed (2)
   Start at  13:19:38
   Duration  122ms
```

When we run the test command, the test runner matches all files with a *test.jsx* suffix. Successful tests are displayed in green, failed tests in red. The interactive test script watches your tests and source code and executes tests when the files change. Vitest also provides a few interactive commands (press "h" to see all of them), such as pressing "f" to run failed tests and "a" for running all tests. Let's see how this looks for a failed test:

src/App.test.jsx

```
import { describe, it, expect } from 'vitest';

describe('something truthy and falsy', () => {
  it('true to be true', () => {
    expect(true).toBe(true);
  });

  it('false to be false', () => {
    expect(false).toBe(true);
  });
});
```

The tests run again, and the command line output shows a failed test in red:

Command Line

```
AssertionError: expected false to be true // Object.is equality

- Expected
+ Received

- true
+ false

src/App.test.jsx:9:19
  7|
  8|    it('false to be false', () => {
  9|        expect(false).toBe(true);
   |                      ^
 10|    });
 11| });

 Test Files  1 failed (1)
      Tests  1 failed | 1 passed (2)
   Start at  13:20:44
   Duration  124ms

 FAIL  Tests failed. Watching for file changes...
       press h to show help, press q to quit
```

Familiarize yourself with this test output, because it shows all failed tests, as well as information on why they failed. Using this information, you can fix certain parts of your code until all tests run green. Next, we'll cover *test assertions*, two of which we've already used with Vitest's expect function. An assertion works by expecting value on the left side (expect) to match a value on the right side (toBe). toBe is only one of many available assertive functions provided by Vitest.

src/App.test.jsx

```
import { describe, it, expect } from 'vitest';

describe('something truthy and falsy', () => {
  it('true to be true', () => {
    expect(true).toBeTruthy();
  });

  it('false to be false', () => {
    expect(false).toBeFalsy();
  });
});
```

Once you start testing, it's a good practice to keep two command line interfaces open: one for watching your tests (npm run test) and one for developing your application (npm run dev). If you are using source control like git, you may want to have even one more command line interface for adding your source code to the repository.

Exercises:

- Compare your source code against the author's source code[294].
  - Recap all the source code changes from this section[295].
- Read more about Vitest[296].

Unit Testing: Functions

A unit test is generally used to test components or functions in isolation. For functions, unit tests are for input and output; for components, we test props, callback handlers communicating to the outside, or the output of the components. Before we can perform a unit test on our *src/App.jsx* file, we must export components and functions like the reducer from our *src/App.jsx* file with a named export:

---

[294]https://bit.ly/3O5SDWL
[295]https://bit.ly/3tRdxSH
[296]https://vitest.dev/

src/App.jsx

```
. . .

export default App;

export { storiesReducer, SearchForm, InputWithLabel, List, Item };
```

The exercises at the end of this chapter will cover all the remaining tests you should consider performing. For now, we can import all the components and reducers in our *src/App.test.jsx* file and we will focus on the reducer test first. We are also importing React here, because we have to include it whenever we test React components:

src/App.test.jsx

```
import { describe, it, expect } from 'vitest';

import App, {
  storiesReducer,
  Item,
  List,
  SearchForm,
  InputWithLabel,
} from './App';
```

Before we unit test our first React component, we'll cover how to test just a JavaScript function. The best candidate for this test use case is the storiesReducer function and one of its actions. Let's define some test data and the test suite for the reducer test:

src/App.test.jsx

```
. . .

const storyOne = {
  title: 'React',
  url: 'https://reactjs.org/',
  author: 'Jordan Walke',
  num_comments: 3,
  points: 4,
  objectID: 0,
};

const storyTwo = {
  title: 'Redux',
```

```
  url: 'https://redux.js.org/',
  author: 'Dan Abramov, Andrew Clark',
  num_comments: 2,
  points: 5,
  objectID: 1,
};

const stories = [storyOne, storyTwo];

describe('storiesReducer', () => {
  it('removes a story from all stories', () => {

  });
});
```

If you extrapolate the test cases, there should be one test case per reducer action. We will focus on a single action, which you can use to perform the rest as exercise yourself. The reducer function accepts a state and an action, and then returns a new state, so all reducer tests essentially follow the same pattern:

src/App.test.jsx

```
...

describe('storiesReducer', () => {
  it('removes a story from all stories', () => {
    const action = // TODO: some action
    const state = // TODO: some current state

    const newState = storiesReducer(state, action);

    const expectedState = // TODO: the expected state

    expect(newState).toBe(expectedState);
  });
});
```

For our case, we define action, state, and expected state according to our reducer. The expected state will have one less story, which was removed as it passed to the reducer as action:

src/App.test.jsx

```
describe('storiesReducer', () => {
  it('removes a story from all stories', () => {
    const action = { type: 'REMOVE_STORY', payload: storyOne };
    const state = { data: stories, isLoading: false, isError: false };

    const newState = storiesReducer(state, action);

    const expectedState = {
      data: [storyTwo],
      isLoading: false,
      isError: false,
    };

    expect(newState).toBe(expectedState);
  });
});
```

This test still fails because we are using toBe instead of toStrictEqual. The toBe assertive function makes a strict comparison like newState === expectedState. The content of the objects are the same, however, their object references are not the same. We use toStrictEqual instead of toBe to limit our comparison to the object's content:

src/App.test.jsx

```
describe('storiesReducer', () => {
  it('removes a story from all stories', () => {
    const action = { type: 'REMOVE_STORY', payload: storyOne };
    const state = { data: stories, isLoading: false, isError: false };

    const newState = storiesReducer(state, action);

    const expectedState = {
      data: [storyTwo],
      isLoading: false,
      isError: false,
    };

    expect(newState).toStrictEqual(expectedState);
  });
});
```

There is always the decision to make for JavaScript objects whether you want to make a strict comparison or just a content comparison. Most often you only want to have a content comparison here, hence use `toStrictEqual`. For JavaScript primitives though, like strings or booleans, you can still use `toBe`. Also note that there is a `toEqual` function which works slightly different[297] than `toStrictEqual`.

We continue to make adjustments until the reducer test turns green, which is really testing a JavaScript function with a certain input and expecting a certain output. We haven't done any testing regarding React components yet.

Remember, a reducer function will always follow the same test pattern: given a state and action, we expect the following new state. Every action of the reducer could be another test case in our reducer's test suite, so consider using the exercises as a way to move through your entire source code.

Exercises:

- Compare your source code against the author's source code[298].
  - Recap all the source code changes from this section[299].
- Continue to write a test case for every reducer action and its state transition.
- Read more about Vitest's assertive functions[300] like `toBe` and `toStrictEqual`.

Unit Testing: Components

We tested our first function in JavaScript with Vitest in the previous section. Next, we'll test our first React component in isolation with a unit test. Therefore we have to tell Vitest about the headless browser environment where we want to render React components, because the test will not start an actual browser for us. However, the HTML that's getting rendered with a React component has to end up somewhere (e.g. headless browser) to make it accessible for testing. The most popular way to perform this task is installing jsdom[301] which acts like a headless browser for us:

Command Line

```
npm install jsdom --save-dev
```

Then we can include it to the Vite configuration file:

[297]https://bit.ly/3jlPpii
[298]https://bit.ly/47WVUPn
[299]https://bit.ly/47JTgMq
[300]https://bit.ly/3xVJbwZ
[301]https://bit.ly/3LJrExK

vite.config.js

```
import { defineConfig } from 'vite';
import react from '@vitejs/plugin-react';

// https://vitejs.dev/config/
export default defineConfig({
  plugins: [react()],
  test: {
    environment: 'jsdom',
  },
});
```

In addition, we will render React components in tests with a library called react-testing-library (RTL). We need to install it too:

Command Line

```
npm install @testing-library/react @testing-library/jest-dom --save-dev
```

Afterward, we create a new file for a general testing setup:

Command Line

```
mkdir tests
cd tests
touch setup.js
```

And reference it in Vite's configuration file:

vite.config.js

```
import { defineConfig } from 'vite';
import react from '@vitejs/plugin-react';

// https://vitejs.dev/config/
export default defineConfig({
  plugins: [react()],
  test: {
    environment: 'jsdom',
    setupFiles: './tests/setup.js',
  },
});
```

Last, include the following implementation details in the new setup file for our tests:

tests/setup.js

```
import { expect, afterEach } from 'vitest';
import { cleanup } from '@testing-library/react';
import * as matchers from "@testing-library/jest-dom/matchers";

expect.extend(matchers);

afterEach(() => {
  cleanup();
});
```

Essentially Vitest's `expect` method gets extended by more methods given from RTL. We will use these methods (e.g. `toBeInTheDocument`) in our tests soonish. Now we can finally import the following functions from React Testing Library which are used for component tests:

src/App.test.jsx

```
import { describe, it, expect } from 'vitest';
import {
  render,
  screen,
  fireEvent,
  waitFor,
} from '@testing-library/react';

...
```

Start with the Item component, where we assert whether it renders all expected properties based on its given props. Based on the input (read: props), we are asserting an output (rendered HTML). We'll use RTL's `render` function in each test to render a React component. In this case, we render the Item component as an element and pass it an `item` object – one of our previously defined stories – as props:

src/App.test.jsx

```
...

const storyOne = { ... };

const storyTwo = { ... };

const stories = [storyOne, storyTwo];

describe('storiesReducer', () => {
```

```
    . . .
});


describe('Item', () => {
  it('renders all properties', () => {
    render(<Item item={storyOne} />);
  });
});
```

After rendering it, we didn't do any testing yet (the tests are turning out green though, because there was no failed test in the test file), so we can use the debug function from RTL's screen object to output on the command line what has been rendered in jsdom's environment:

src/App.test.jsx

```
describe('Item', () => {
  it('renders all properties', () => {
    render(<Item item={storyOne} />);

    screen.debug();
  });
});
```

Run the tests with npm run test, and you'll see the output from the debug function. It prints all your component's and child component's HTML elements. The output should be similar to the following:

Command Line

```
<body>
  <div>
    <li>
      <span>
        <a
          href="https://reactjs.org/"
        >
          React
        </a>
      </span>
      <span>
        Jordan Walke
      </span>
      <span>
        3
      </span>
```

```
      <span>
        4
      </span>
      <span>
        <button
          type="button"
        >
          Dismiss
        </button>
      </span>
    </li>
  </div>
</body>
```

Here you should form the habit of using RTL's debug function whenever you render a new component in a React component test. The function gives a useful overview of what is rendered and informs the best way to proceed with testing. Based on the current output, we can start with our first assertion. RTL's screen object provides a function called getByText, one of many search functions:

src/App.test.jsx

```
describe('Item', () => {
  it('renders all properties', () => {
    render(<Item item={storyOne} />);

    expect(screen.getByText('Jordan Walke')).toBeInTheDocument();
    expect(screen.getByText('React')).toHaveAttribute(
      'href',
      'https://reactjs.org/'
    );
  });
});
```

For the two assertions, we use the two assertive functions toBeInTheDocument and toHaveAttribute (both needed the expect extension from the *tests/setup.js* file). These are to verify an element with the text "Jordan Walke" is in the document, and the presence of an element with the text "React" with a specific href attribute value. Over time, you will see more of these assertive functions being used.

RTL's getByText search function finds the one element with the visible texts "Jordan Walke" and "React". We can use the getAllByText equivalent to find more than one element. Similar equivalents exist for other search functions.

The getByText function returns the element with a text that users can see, which relates to the real-world use of the application. Note that getByText is not the only search function, though. Another highly-used search function is the getByRole or getAllByRole function:

src/App.test.jsx

```
describe('Item', () => {
  it('renders all properties', () => {
    ...
  });

  it('renders a clickable dismiss button', () => {
    render(<Item item={storyOne} />);

    expect(screen.getByRole('button')).toBeInTheDocument();
  });
});
```

The getByRole function is usually used to retrieve elements by aria-label attributes[302]. However, there are also implicit roles on HTML elements[303] – like "button" for a button HTML element. Thus you can select elements not only by visible text, but also by their (implicit) accessibility role with React Testing Library. A neat feature of getRoleBy is that it suggests roles if you provide a role that's not available[304].

src/App.test.jsx

```
describe('Item', () => {
  it('renders all properties', () => {
    ...
  });

  it('renders a clickable dismiss button', () => {
    render(<Item item={storyOne} />);

    screen.getByRole('');

    // expect(screen.getByRole('button')).toBeInTheDocument();
  });
});
```

Which should output something similar to the following on the command line:

---

[302]https://mzl.la/49oo8U0
[303]https://mzl.la/3n7SgN7
[304]https://bit.ly/3pnPXrQ

Command Line

```
TestingLibraryElementError:
Unable to find an accessible element with the role ""
Here are the accessible roles:

  listitem:
  Name "":
  <li />

  link:
  Name "React":
  <a
    href="https://reactjs.org/"
  />

  button:
  Name "Dismiss":
  <button
    type="button"
  />
```

Both, getByText and getByRole are RTL's most widely used search functions. We can continue here by asserting not only that everything is *in the document*, but also by asserting whether our events work as expected. For example, the Item component's button element can be clicked and we want to verify that the callback handler gets called. Therefore, we are using Vitest for creating a mocked function which we provide as a callback handler to the Item component. Then, after firing a click event with React Testing Library on the button, we want to assert that the callback handler function has been called:

src/App.test.jsx

```
import { describe, it, expect, vi } from 'vitest';

...

describe('Item', () => {
  it('renders all properties', () => {
    ...
  });

  it('renders a clickable dismiss button', () => {
    ...
  });
```

```
  it('clicking the dismiss button calls the callback handler', () => {
    const handleRemoveItem = vi.fn();

    render(<Item item={storyOne} onRemoveItem={handleRemoveItem} />);

    fireEvent.click(screen.getByRole('button'));

    expect(handleRemoveItem).toHaveBeenCalledTimes(1);
  });
});
```

Vitest lets us pass a test-specific function to the Item component as a prop. These test-specific functions are called **spy**, **stub**, or **mock**; each is used for different test scenarios. The vi.fn() returns us a *mock* for the actual function, which lets us capture when it's called. As a result, we can use Vitest's assertions like toHaveBeenCalledTimes, which lets us assert a number of times the function has been called; and toHaveBeenCalledWith, to verify arguments that are passed to it.

Every time we want to mock a JavaScript function, whether it has been called or whether it received certain arguments, we can use Vitest's helper function to create a mocked function. Then, after invoking this function with RTL's fireEvent object's function, we can assert that the provided callback handler – which is the mocked function – has been called one time.

In the last exercise we tested the Item component's input and output via rendering assertions and callback handler assertions. We are not testing real state changes yet, however, as there is no actual item removed from the DOM after clicking the "Dismiss"-button. The logic to remove the item from the list is in the App component, but we are only testing the Item component in isolation. Sometimes it's just useful to test whether a single block works, before testing everything all together. We will test the actual implementation logic for removing an Item when we cover the App component later.

For now, the SearchForm component uses the InputWithLabel component as a child component. We will make this to our next test case. As before, we will start by rendering the component, here the parent component, and providing all the essential props:

src/App.test.jsx

```
. . .

describe('SearchForm', () => {
  const searchFormProps = {
    searchTerm: 'React',
    onSearchInput: vi.fn(),
    onSearchSubmit: vi.fn(),
  };
```

```
  it('renders the input field with its value', () => {
    render(<SearchForm {...searchFormProps} />);

    screen.debug();
  });
});
```

Again, we start with the debugging. After evaluating what renders on the command line, we can make the first assertion for the SearchForm component. With input fields in place, the getByDisplayValue search function from RTL is the perfect candidate to return the input field as an element:

src/App.test.jsx

```
describe('SearchForm', () => {
  const searchFormProps = { ... };

  it('renders the input field with its value', () => {
    render(<SearchForm {...searchFormProps} />);

    expect(screen.getByDisplayValue('React')).toBeInTheDocument();
  });
});
```

Since the HTML input element is rendered with a default value, we can use the default value (here: "React"), which is the displayed value in our test assertion. If the input element doesn't have a default value, the application could show a placeholder with the placeholder HTML attribute on the input field. Then we'd use another function from RTL called getByPlaceholderText, which is used for searching an element with a placeholder text.

Because the debug information presented multiple options to query the HTML, we could continue with one more test to assert the rendered label:

src/App.test.jsx

```
describe('SearchForm', () => {
  const searchFormProps = { ... };

  it('renders the input field with its value', () => {
    ...
  });

  it('renders the correct label', () => {
    render(<SearchForm {...searchFormProps} />);
```

```
    expect(screen.getByLabelText(/Search/)).toBeInTheDocument();
  });
});
```

The getByLabelText search function allows us to find an element by a label in a form. This is useful for components that render multiple labels and HTML controls. However, you may have noticed we used a regular expression[305] here. If we used a string instead, the colon for "Search:" must be included. By using a regular expression, we are matching strings that include the "Search" string, which makes finding elements much more efficient. For this reason, you may find yourself using regular expressions instead of strings quite often.

Anyway, perhaps it would be more interesting to test the interactive parts of the SearchForm component. Since our callback handlers, which are passed as props to the SearchForm component, are already mocked with Vitest, we can assert whether these functions get called appropriately:

src/App.test.jsx

```
describe('SearchForm', () => {
  const searchFormProps = {
    searchTerm: 'React',
    onSearchInput: vi.fn(),
    onSearchSubmit: vi.fn(),
  };

  ...

  it('calls onSearchInput on input field change', () => {
    render(<SearchForm {...searchFormProps} />);

    fireEvent.change(screen.getByDisplayValue('React'), {
      target: { value: 'Redux' },
    });

    expect(searchFormProps.onSearchInput).toHaveBeenCalledTimes(1);
  });

  it('calls onSearchSubmit on button submit click', () => {
    render(<SearchForm {...searchFormProps} />);

    fireEvent.submit(screen.getByRole('button'));

    expect(searchFormProps.onSearchSubmit).toHaveBeenCalledTimes(1);
```

---

[305]https://mzl.la/3CdDjiZ

```
  });
});
```

Similar to the Item component, we tested input (props) and output (callback handler) for the Search-Form component. The difference is that the SearchForm component renders a child component called InputWithLabel. If you check the debug output, you'll likely notice that React Testing Library just renders the whole component tree for both components. This happens because the end-user wouldn't care about the component tree either, but only about the HTML that is getting displayed. So the React Testing Library outputs all the HTML that matters for the user and thus the test.

All the callback handler tests for Item and SearchForm component verify only whether the functions have been called. No React re-rendering occurs, because all the components are tested in isolation without state management, which solely happens in the App component. Real testing with RTL starts further up the component tree, where state changes and side-effects can be evaluated. Therefore, let me introduce integration testing next.

Exercises:

- Compare your source code against the author's source code[306].
  - Recap all the source code changes from this section[307].
- Read more about React Testing Library[308].
  - Read more about search functions[309].
- Use toHaveBeenCalledWith next to toHaveBeenCalledTimes to make your assertions more bullet proof.
- Add tests for your List and InputWithLabel components.

Integration Testing: Component

React Testing Library adheres to a single core philosophy: instead of testing implementation details of React components, it tests how users interact with the application and if it works as expected. This becomes especially powerful for integration tests.

We'll need to provide some data before we test the App component, since it makes requests for data from a remote API after its initial render. Because we are using axios for the data fetching in the App component, we'll have to mock it with Vitest at the top of the testing file:

---

[306]https://bit.ly/48vMWtj
[307]https://bit.ly/3O8yHCu
[308]https://bit.ly/30KueQH
[309]https://bit.ly/3jjUw2t

src/App.test.jsx

```
. . .

import axios from 'axios';

. . .

vi.mock('axios');

. . .
```

Next, implement the data you want to be returned from the mocked API request with a JavaScript Promise, and use it for the axios mock. Afterward, we can render our component and assume the correct data is mocked for our API request:

src/App.test.jsx

```
. . .

describe('App', () => {
  it('succeeds fetching data', () => {
    const promise = Promise.resolve({
      data: {
        hits: stories,
      },
    });

    axios.get.mockImplementationOnce(() => promise);

    render(<App />);

    screen.debug();
  });
});
```

Now we'll use React Testing Library's waitFor helper function to wait until the promise resolves after the component's initial render. With async/await, we can implement this like synchronous code. The debug function from RTL is useful because it outputs the App component's elements before and after the request:

src/App.test.jsx

```
describe('App', () => {
  it('succeeds fetching data', async () => {
    const promise = Promise.resolve({
      data: {
        hits: stories,
      },
    });

    axios.get.mockImplementationOnce(() => promise);

    render(<App />);

    screen.debug();

    await waitFor(async () => await promise);

    screen.debug();
  });
});
```

In the debug's output, we see the loading indicator renders for the first debug function, but not the second. This is because the data fetching and component re-render complete after we resolve the promise in our test with waitFor. Let's assert the loading indicator for this case:

src/App.test.jsx

```
describe('App', () => {
  it('succeeds fetching data', async () => {
    const promise = Promise.resolve({
      data: {
        hits: stories,
      },
    });

    axios.get.mockImplementationOnce(() => promise);

    render(<App />);

    expect(screen.queryByText(/Loading/)).toBeInTheDocument();

    await waitFor(async () => await promise);
```

```
      expect(screen.queryByText(/Loading/)).toBeNull();
  });
});
```

Because we're testing for a returned element that is absent, this time we use RTL's queryByText instead of the getByText function. Using getByText in this instance would produce an error, because the element can't be found; but with queryByText the value just returns null.

Again, we're using a regular expression /Loading/ instead of a string 'Loading'. To use a string, we'd have to explicitly use 'Loading ...' instead of 'Loading'. With a regular expression, we don't need to provide the whole string, we just need to match a part of it.

Next, we can assert whether or not our fetched data gets rendered as expected:

src/App.test.jsx

```
describe('App', () => {
  it('succeeds fetching data', async () => {
    const promise = Promise.resolve({
      data: {
        hits: stories,
      },
    });

    axios.get.mockImplementationOnce(() => promise);

    render(<App />);

    expect(screen.queryByText(/Loading/)).toBeInTheDocument();

    await waitFor(async () => await promise);

    expect(screen.queryByText(/Loading/)).toBeNull();

    expect(screen.getByText('React')).toBeInTheDocument();
    expect(screen.getByText('Redux')).toBeInTheDocument();
    expect(screen.getAllByText('Dismiss').length).toBe(2);
  });
});
```

The happy path[310] for the data fetching is tested now. Similarly, we can test the unhappy path in case of a failed API request. The promise needs to reject and the error should be caught with a try/catch block:

[310]https://bit.ly/3jiAbuB

src/App.test.jsx

```
describe('App', () => {
  it('succeeds fetching data', async () => {
    ...
  });

  it('fails fetching data', async () => {
    const promise = Promise.reject();

    axios.get.mockImplementationOnce(() => promise);

    render(<App />);

    expect(screen.getByText(/Loading/)).toBeInTheDocument();

    try {
      await waitFor(async () => await promise);
    } catch (error) {
      expect(screen.queryByText(/Loading/)).toBeNull();
      expect(screen.queryByText(/went wrong/)).toBeInTheDocument();
    }
  });
});
```

There may be some confusion about when to use getBy or the queryBy search variants. As a rule of thumb, use getBy for single elements, and getAllBy for multiple elements. If you are checking for elements that aren't present, use queryBy (or queryAllBy). In this code, I preferred using queryBy for the sake of alignment and readability.

Now we know the initial data fetching works for our App component, so we can move to testing user interactions. We have only tested user actions in the child components thus far, by firing events without any state and side-effect. Next, we'll remove an item from the list after the data has been fetched successfully. Since the item with "Jordan Walke" is the first rendered item in the list, it gets removed if we click the first "Dismiss"-button:

src/App.test.jsx

```
describe('App', () => {

  ...

  it('removes a story', async () => {
    const promise = Promise.resolve({
      data: {
        hits: stories,
      },
    });

    axios.get.mockImplementationOnce(() => promise);

    render(<App />);

    await waitFor(async () => await promise);

    expect(screen.getAllByText('Dismiss').length).toBe(2);
    expect(screen.getByText('Jordan Walke')).toBeInTheDocument();

    fireEvent.click(screen.getAllByText('Dismiss')[0]);

    expect(screen.getAllByText('Dismiss').length).toBe(1);
    expect(screen.queryByText('Jordan Walke')).toBeNull();
  });
});
```

To test the search feature, we set up the mocking differently, because we're handling initial request, plus another request once the user searches for more stories by a specific search term:

src/App.test.jsx

```
describe('App', () => {

  ...

  it('searches for specific stories', async () => {
    const reactPromise = Promise.resolve({
      data: {
        hits: stories,
      },
    });
```

```
const anotherStory = {
  title: 'JavaScript',
  url: 'https://en.wikipedia.org/wiki/JavaScript',
  author: 'Brendan Eich',
  num_comments: 15,
  points: 10,
  objectID: 3,
};

const javascriptPromise = Promise.resolve({
  data: {
    hits: [anotherStory],
  },
});

axios.get.mockImplementation((url) => {
  if (url.includes('React')) {
    return reactPromise;
  }

  if (url.includes('JavaScript')) {
    return javascriptPromise;
  }

  throw Error();
});
});
});
```

Instead of mocking the request once with Vitest (mockImplementationOnce), now we mock multiple requests (mockImplementation). Depending on the incoming URL, the request either returns the initial list ("React"-related stories), or the new list ("JavaScript"-related stories). If we provide an incorrect URL to the request, the test throws an error for confirmation. As before, let's render the App component:

src/App.test.jsx

```
describe('App', () => {

  ...

  it('searches for specific stories', async () => {
    const reactPromise = Promise.resolve({ ... });

    const anotherStory = { ... };

    const javascriptPromise = Promise.resolve({ ... });

    axios.get.mockImplementation((url) => {
      ...
    });

    // Initial Render

    render(<App />);

    // First Data Fetching

    await waitFor(async () => await reactPromise);

    expect(screen.queryByDisplayValue('React')).toBeInTheDocument();
    expect(screen.queryByDisplayValue('JavaScript')).toBeNull();

    expect(screen.queryByText('Jordan Walke')).toBeInTheDocument();
    expect(
      screen.queryByText('Dan Abramov, Andrew Clark')
    ).toBeInTheDocument();
    expect(screen.queryByText('Brendan Eich')).toBeNull();
  });
});
```

We are resolving the first promise for the initial render. We expect the input field to render "React", and the two items in the list to render the creators of React and Redux. We also make sure that no stories related to JavaScript are rendered yet. Next, change the input field's value by firing an event, and asserting that the new value is rendered from the App component through all its child components in the actual input field:

src/App.test.jsx

```
describe('App', () => {

  ...

  it('searches for specific stories', async () => {

    ...

    expect(screen.queryByText('Jordan Walke')).toBeInTheDocument();
    expect(
      screen.queryByText('Dan Abramov, Andrew Clark')
    ).toBeInTheDocument();
    expect(screen.queryByText('Brendan Eich')).toBeNull();

    // User Interaction -> Search

    fireEvent.change(screen.queryByDisplayValue('React'), {
      target: {
        value: 'JavaScript',
      },
    });

    expect(screen.queryByDisplayValue('React')).toBeNull();
    expect(
      screen.queryByDisplayValue('JavaScript')
    ).toBeInTheDocument();
  });
});
```

Lastly, we can submit this search request by firing a submit event with the button. The new search term is used from the App component's state, so the new URL searches for JavaScript-related stories that we have mocked before:

src/App.test.jsx

```
describe('App', () => {

  ...

  it('searches for specific stories', async () => {

    ...

    expect(screen.queryByDisplayValue('React')).toBeNull();
    expect(
      screen.queryByDisplayValue('JavaScript')
    ).toBeInTheDocument();

    fireEvent.submit(screen.queryByText('Submit'));

    // Second Data Fetching

    await waitFor(async () => await javascriptPromise);

    expect(screen.queryByText('Jordan Walke')).toBeNull();
    expect(
      screen.queryByText('Dan Abramov, Andrew Clark')
    ).toBeNull();
    expect(screen.queryByText('Brendan Eich')).toBeInTheDocument();
  });
});
```

Brendan Eich is rendered as the creator of JavaScript, while the creators of React and Redux are removed. This test depicts an entire test scenario in one test case. We can move through each step – initial fetching, changing the input field value, submitting the form, and retrieving new data from the API – with the tools we've used.

React Testing Library with Vitest is the most popular library combination for React testing. RTL provides relevant testing tools, while Vitest has a general testing framework for test suites, test cases, assertions, and mocking capabilities. If you need an alternative to RTL, consider trying Enzyme[311] by Airbnb.

Exercises:

- Compare your source code against the author's source code[312].

---

[311]https://www.robinwieruch.de/react-testing-jest-enzyme/
[312]https://bit.ly/3O8zp2C

> – Recap all the source code changes from this section[313].
- Read more about React Testing Library in React[314].
- Read more about E2E tests in React[315].
- While you continue with the upcoming sections, keep your tests green and add new tests when needed.

Snapshot Testing

Snapshot tests as a more lightweight way to test React components and their structure. Essentially a snapshot test creates an instance of your rendered component's output as HTML elements and their structure. This snapshot is compared to the same snapshot in the next test to give more output on how the rendered component changed and show why any tests failed in the difference. You can accept or deny any differences in your source code until the component functions as intended.

Snapshot tests are lightweight, with less focus on the implementation details of the component. Let's perform a snapshot test for our SearchForm component:

src/App.test.jsx

```
describe('SearchForm', () => {

  ...

  it('renders snapshot', () => {
    const { container } = render(<SearchForm {...searchFormProps} />);
    expect(container.firstChild).toMatchSnapshot();
  });
});
```

Run the tests with `npm run test` and you'll see a new *src/_snapshots_* folder has been created in your project folder. Similar to RTL's `debug` function, there's a snapshot of your rendered SearchForm component as an HTML element structure in the file. Next, head to *src/App.jsx* file and change the HTML. For example, try removing the bold text from the SearchForm component:

---

[313]https://bit.ly/3U85PhI
[314]https://www.robinwieruch.de/react-testing-library/
[315]https://www.robinwieruch.de/react-testing-cypress/

src/App.jsx

```
const SearchForm = ({
  searchTerm,
  onSearchInput,
  onSearchSubmit,
}) => (
  <form onSubmit={onSearchSubmit}>
    <InputWithLabel
      id="search"
      value={searchTerm}
      isFocused
      onInputChange={onSearchInput}
    >
      Search:
    </InputWithLabel>

    <button type="submit" disabled={!searchTerm}>
      Submit
    </button>
  </form>
);
```

After the next test, the command line should look similar to the following:

Command Line

```
- Expected   - 3
+ Received   + 1

      <label
        for="search"
      >
-       <strong>
-         Search:
-       </strong>
+       Search:
      </label>


Snapshots  1 failed
```

This is a typical case for a breaking snapshot test. When a component's HTML structure is changed unintentionally, the snapshot test informs us on the command line. To fix it, we would go into the *src/App.jsx* file and edit the SearchForm component. For intentional changes, press "u" on the command line for interactive tests and a new snapshot will be created. Try it and see how the snapshot file in your *src/_snapshots_* folder changes.

Vitest stores snapshots in a folder so it can validate the difference against future snapshot tests. Users can share these snapshots across teams using version control platforms like git. This is how we make sure the DOM stays the same.

Snapshot tests are useful for setting up tests quickly in React, though it's best to avoid using them exclusively. Instead, use snapshot tests for components that don't update often, are less complex, and where it's easier to compare component results.

Exercises:

- Compare your source code against the author's source code[316].
    - Recap all the source code changes from this section[317].
- Add one snapshot test for each of all the other components and check the content of your *src/_snapshots_/* folder.
- Optional: Leave feedback for this section[318].

---

[316]https://bit.ly/47FyXjl
[317]https://bit.ly/3SroKCV
[318]https://forms.gle/tMJyXvxS1AmRvSUU9

React Project Structure

With multiple React components in one file, you might wonder why we didn't put components into different files from the start. We already have multiple components in the *src/App.jsx* file that can be defined in their own files/folders (sometimes also called modules). For learning, it's more practical to keep these components in one place. Once your application grows, consider splitting these components into multiple files/folders/modules so it scales properly. Before we restructure our React project, recap JavaScript's import and export statements[319], because importing and exporting files are two fundamental concepts in JavaScript you should learn before React.

It's important to note that there's no right way to structure a React application, as they evolve naturally along with the project's requirements. We'll complete a simple refactoring for this project's folder/file structure for the sake of learning about the process. Afterward, there will be an important article as exercise about the folder/file organizations of React projects.

On the command line in your project's folder, create the following files for all of our components in the *src/* folder:

Command Line

```
touch src/List.jsx src/InputWithLabel.jsx src/SearchForm.jsx
```

Move every component from the *src/App.jsx* file in its own file, except for the List component which has to share its place with the Item component in the *src/List.jsx* file. Then in every file make sure to import React and to export the component which needs to be used from the file. For example, in *src/List.jsx* file:

src/List.jsx

```
const List = ({ list, onRemoveItem }) => (
  <ul>
    {list.map((item) => (
      <Item
        key={item.objectID}
        item={item}
        onRemoveItem={onRemoveItem}
      />
    ))}
  </ul>
);

const Item = ({ item, onRemoveItem }) => (
  <li>
    <span>
```

---
[319]https://www.robinwieruch.de/javascript-import-export/

```
        <a href={item.url}>{item.title}</a>
      </span>
      <span>{item.author}</span>
      <span>{item.num_comments}</span>
      <span>{item.points}</span>
      <span>
        <button type="button" onClick={() => onRemoveItem(item)}>
          Dismiss
        </button>
      </span>
    </li>
);
```

```
export { List };
```

Since only the List component uses the Item component, we can keep it in the same file. If this changes because the Item component is used elsewhere, we can give the Item component its own file. Next, the InputWithLabel component gets its dedicated file too:

src/InputWithLabel.jsx

```
import * as React from 'react';

const InputWithLabel = ({
  id,
  value,
  type = 'text',
  onInputChange,
  isFocused,
  children,
}) => {
  const inputRef = React.useRef();

  React.useEffect(() => {
    if (isFocused && inputRef.current) {
      inputRef.current.focus();
    }
  }, [isFocused]);

  return (
    <>
      <label htmlFor={id}>{children}</label>
       
      <input
```

```
        ref={inputRef}
        id={id}
        type={type}
        value={value}
        onChange={onInputChange}
      />
    </>
  );
};
```

```
export { InputWithLabel };
```

The SearchForm component in the *src/SearchForm.jsx* file must import the InputWithLabel component. Like the Item component, we could have left the InputWithLabel component next to the SearchForm; but our goal is to make InputWithLabel component reusable with other components:

src/SearchForm.jsx

```
import { InputWithLabel } from './InputWithLabel';

const SearchForm = ({
  searchTerm,
  onSearchInput,
  onSearchSubmit,
}) => (
  <form onSubmit={onSearchSubmit}>
    <InputWithLabel
      id="search"
      value={searchTerm}
      isFocused
      onInputChange={onSearchInput}
    >
      <strong>Search:</strong>
    </InputWithLabel>

    <button type="submit" disabled={!searchTerm}>
      Submit
    </button>
  </form>
);
```

```
export { SearchForm };
```

The App component has to import all the components it needs to render. It doesn't need to import InputWithLabel, because it's only used for the SearchForm component.

src/App.jsx

```
import * as React from 'react';
import axios from 'axios';

import { SearchForm } from './SearchForm';
import { List } from './List';

...

const App = () => {
  ...
};

export default App;
```

Components that are used in other components now have their own file. If a component should be used as a reusable component (e.g. InputWithLabel), it receives its own file. Only if a component (e.g. Item) is dedicated to another component (e.g. List) do we keep it in the same file. From here, there are several strategies to structure your folder/file hierarchy. One scenario is to create a folder for every component:

Project Structure

```
- List/
-- index.jsx
- SearchForm/
-- index.jsx
- InputWithLabel/
-- index.jsx
```

The *index.jsx* file holds the implementation details for the component, while other files in the same folder have different responsibilities like styling, testing, and types:

Project Structure

```
- List/
-- index.jsx
-- style.css
-- test.js
-- types.js
```

If using CSS-in-JS, where no CSS file is needed, one could still have a separate *style.js* file for all the styled components:

Project Structure

```
- List/
-- index.jsx
-- style.js
-- test.js
-- types.js
```

Sometimes we'll need to move from a **technical-oriented folder structure** to a **domain-oriented folder structure**, especially once the project grows. Universal *shared/* folder is shared across domain specific components:

Project Structure

```
- Messages.jsx
- Users.jsx
- shared/
-- Button.jsx
-- Input.jsx
```

If you scale this to the deeper level folder structure, each component will have its own folder in a domain-oriented project structure as well:

Project Structure

```
- Messages/
-- index.jsx
-- style.css
-- test.js
-- types.js
- Users/
-- index.jsx
-- style.css
-- test.js
```

```
-- types.js
- shared/
-- Button/
--- index.jsx
--- style.css
--- test.js
--- types.js
-- Input/
--- index.jsx
--- style.css
--- test.js
--- types.js
```

There are many ways on how to structure your React project from small to large project: simple
to complex folder structure; one-level nested to two-level nested folder nesting; dedicated folders
for styling, types, and testing next to implementation logic. There is no right way for folder/file
structures. However, in the exercises, you will find my 5 steps approach to structure a React project.
After all, a project's requirements evolve over time and so should its structure. If keeping all assets
in one file feels right, then there is no rule against it.

Exercises:

- Compare your source code against the author's source code[320].
  - Recap all the source code changes from this section[321].
- Read more about React Folder Structures[322].
- Keep the current folder structure if you feel confident. The ongoing sections will omit it, only
  using the *src/App.jsx* file.
- Optional: Leave feedback for this section[323].

[320]https://bit.ly/3vAhuLO
[321]https://bit.ly/3vJDx2U
[322]https://www.robinwieruch.de/react-folder-structure/
[323]https://forms.gle/yLzszsmtdB1DQBCe7

Real World React (Advanced)

We've covered most of React's fundamentals, its legacy features, and techniques for maintaining applications. Now it's time to dive into developing real-world React features. Each of the following sections will come with a task. Try to tackle these tasks without the *optional hints* first, but be aware that these are going to be challenging on your first attempt. If you need help, use the *optional hints* or follow the instructions from the section.

Sorting

Task: Working with a list of items often includes interactions that make data more approachable by users. So far, every item was listed with each of its properties. To make it explorable, the list should enable the sorting of each property by title, author, comments, and points in ascending or descending order. Sorting in only one direction is fine, because sorting in the other direction will be part of the next task.

Optional Hints:

- Introduce a new sort state in the App or List component.
- For each property (e.g. `title`, `author`, `points`, `num_comments`) implement an HTML button which sets the sort state for this property.
- Use the sort state to apply an appropriate sort function on the `list`.
- Using a utility library like Lodash[324] for its `sortBy` function is encouraged.

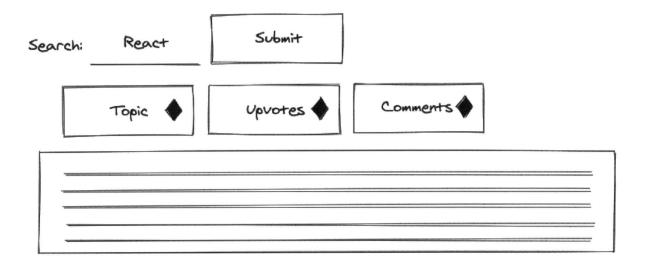

Okay, let's tackle this task! We will treat the list of data like a table. Each row represents an item of the list and each column represents one property of the item. Introducing headers should provide the user more guidance about each column:

---

[324]https://lodash.com

src/App.jsx

```
const List = ({ list, onRemoveItem }) => (
  <ul>
    <li style={{ display: 'flex' }}>
      <span style={{ width: '40%' }}>Title</span>
      <span style={{ width: '30%' }}>Author</span>
      <span style={{ width: '10%' }}>Comments</span>
      <span style={{ width: '10%' }}>Points</span>
      <span style={{ width: '10%' }}>Actions</span>
    </li>

    {list.map((item) => (
      <Item
        key={item.objectID}
        item={item}
        onRemoveItem={onRemoveItem}
      />
    ))}
  </ul>
);
```

We are using inline style for the most basic layout. To match the layout of the header with the rows, give the rows in the Item component a layout as well:

src/App.jsx

```
const Item = ({ item, onRemoveItem }) => (
  <li style={{ display: 'flex' }}>
    <span style={{ width: '40%' }}>
      <a href={item.url}>{item.title}</a>
    </span>
    <span style={{ width: '30%' }}>{item.author}</span>
    <span style={{ width: '10%' }}>{item.num_comments}</span>
    <span style={{ width: '10%' }}>{item.points}</span>
    <span style={{ width: '10%' }}>
      <button type="button" onClick={() => onRemoveItem(item)}>
        Dismiss
      </button>
    </span>
  </li>
);
```

In the ongoing implementation, we will remove the style attributes, because it takes up lots of space and clutters the actual implementation logic (hence extracting it into proper CSS). But I encourage you to keep it for yourself.

The List component will handle the new sort state. This can also be done in the App component, but in the end, only the List component needs it, so we can lift the state directly to it. The sort state initializes with a 'NONE' state, so the list items are displayed in the order they are fetched from the API. Furthermore, we will add a new handler to set the sort state with a sort-specific key:

src/App.jsx

```
const List = ({ list, onRemoveItem }) => {
  const [sort, setSort] = React.useState('NONE');

  const handleSort = (sortKey) => {
    setSort(sortKey);
  };

  return (
    ...
  );
};
```

In the List component's header, buttons can help us to set the sort state for each column/property. An inline handler is used to sneak in the sort-specific key (sortKey). When the button for the "Title" column is clicked, 'TITLE' becomes the new sort state:

src/App.jsx

```
const List = ({ list, onRemoveItem }) => {
  ...

  return (
    <ul>
      <li>
        <span>
          <button type="button" onClick={() => handleSort('TITLE')}>
            Title
          </button>
        </span>
        <span>
          <button type="button" onClick={() => handleSort('AUTHOR')}>
            Author
          </button>
        </span>
```

```
        <span>
          <button type="button" onClick={() => handleSort('COMMENT')}>
            Comments
          </button>
        </span>
        <span>
          <button type="button" onClick={() => handleSort('POINT')}>
            Points
          </button>
        </span>
        <span>Actions</span>
      </li>

      {list.map((item) => ... )}
    </ul>
  );
};
```

The state management for the new feature is implemented, but we don't see anything when our buttons are clicked yet. This happens because the sorting mechanism hasn't been applied to the actual `list`. Sorting an array with JavaScript isn't trivial, because every JavaScript primitive (e.g. string, boolean, number) comes with edge cases when an array is sorted by its properties. We will use a library called Lodash[325] to solve this, which comes with many JavaScript utility functions (e.g. `sortBy`). First, install it via the command line:

Command Line

```
npm install lodash
```

Second, at the top of your file, import the utility function for sorting:

src/App.jsx

```
import * as React from 'react';
import axios from 'axios';
import { sortBy } from 'lodash';

...
```

Third, create a JavaScript object (also called dictionary in this case) with all the possible `sortKey` and sort function mappings. Each specific sort key is mapped to a function that sorts the incoming `list`. Sorting by `'NONE'` returns the unsorted list; sorting by `'POINT'` returns a list and its items sorted by the `points` property, and so on:

---
[325]https://lodash.com

src/App.jsx

```
const SORTS = {
  NONE: (list) => list,
  TITLE: (list) => sortBy(list, 'title'),
  AUTHOR: (list) => sortBy(list, 'author'),
  COMMENT: (list) => sortBy(list, 'num_comments').reverse(),
  POINT: (list) => sortBy(list, 'points').reverse(),
};

const List = ({ list, onRemoveItem }) => {
  ...
};
```

With the sort (sortKey) state and all possible sort variations (SORTS) at our disposal, we can sort the list before mapping it:

src/App.jsx

```
const List = ({ list, onRemoveItem }) => {
  const [sort, setSort] = React.useState('NONE');

  const handleSort = (sortKey) => {
    setSort(sortKey);
  };

  const sortFunction = SORTS[sort];
  const sortedList = sortFunction(list);

  return (
    <ul>
      ...

      {sortedList.map((item) => (
        <Item
          key={item.objectID}
          item={item}
          onRemoveItem={onRemoveItem}
        />
      ))}
    </ul>
  );
};
```

Task's done and here comes the recap: First we extracted the sort function from the dictionary by its sortKey (state), then we applied the function to the list before mapping it to render each Item component. Second, we rendered HTML buttons as header columns to give our users interaction. Then, we added implementation details for each button by changing the sort state. Finally, we used the sort state to sort the actual list.

Exercises:

- Compare your source code against the author's source code[326].
  - Recap all the source code changes from this section[327].
- Read more about Lodash[328].
- Why did we use numeric properties like `points` and `num_comments` for a reverse sort?
- Use your styling skills to give the user feedback about the current active sort. This mechanism can be as straightforward as giving the active sort button a different color.
- Optional: Leave feedback for this section[329].

---

[326]https://bit.ly/3ScYrz4
[327]https://bit.ly/3HruJBg
[328]https://lodash.com
[329]https://forms.gle/GM71SDZZWPQWEwmB7

Reverse Sort

Task: The sort feature works, but the ordering only includes one direction. Implement a reverse sort when a sort button is clicked twice, so it becomes a toggle between normal (ascending) and reverse (descending) sort.

Optional Hints:

- Consider that reverse or normal sort could be just another state (e.g. isReverse) next to the sortKey.
- Set the new state in the handleSort handler based on the previous sort.
- Use the new isReverse state for sorting the list with the sort function from the dictionary with the optionally applied reverse() function from JavaScript arrays.

Let's get to the task. The initial sort direction works for strings, as well as numeric sorts like the reverse sort for JavaScript numbers that arranges them from high to low. Now we need another state to track whether the sort is reversed or normal:

src/App.jsx

```
const List = ({ list, onRemoveItem }) => {
  const [sort, setSort] = React.useState({
    sortKey: 'NONE',
    isReverse: false,
  });

  ...
};
```

Next, give the sort handler logic to see if the incoming sortKey triggers are a normal or reverse sort. If the sortKey is the same as the one in the state, it should be a reverse sort, but only if the sort state wasn't already reversed:

src/App.jsx

```
const List = ({ list, onRemoveItem }) => {
  const [sort, setSort] = React.useState({
    sortKey: 'NONE',
    isReverse: false,
  });

  const handleSort = (sortKey) => {
    const isReverse = sort.sortKey === sortKey && !sort.isReverse;
```

```
      setSort({ sortKey: sortKey, isReverse: isReverse });
  };

  const sortFunction = SORTS[sort.sortKey];
  const sortedList = sortFunction(list);

  return (
    ...
  );
};
```

Lastly, depending on the new `isReverse` state, apply the sort function from the dictionary with or without the built-in JavaScript reverse method for arrays:

src/App.jsx

```
const List = ({ list, onRemoveItem }) => {
  const [sort, setSort] = React.useState({
    sortKey: 'NONE',
    isReverse: false,
  });

  const handleSort = (sortKey) => {
    const isReverse = sort.sortKey === sortKey && !sort.isReverse;

    setSort({ sortKey, isReverse });
  };

  const sortFunction = SORTS[sort.sortKey];
  const sortedList = sort.isReverse
    ? sortFunction(list).reverse()
    : sortFunction(list);

  return (
    ...
  );
};
```

The reverse sort is now operational! Congratulations, you have a fully sortable list now. And by the way: For the object passed to the state updater function, we use what is called a **shorthand object initializer notation**:

Code Playground

```
const firstName = 'Robin';

const user = {
  firstName: firstName,
};

console.log(user);
// { firstName: "Robin" }
```

When the property name in your object is the same as your variable name, you can omit the key/value pair and just write the name:

Code Playground

```
const firstName = 'Robin';

const user = {
  firstName,
};

console.log(user);
// { firstName: "Robin" }
```

If necessary, read more about JavaScript Object Initializers[330].

Exercises:

- Compare your source code against the author's source code[331].
  - Recap all the source code changes from this section[332].
- Consider the drawback of keeping the sort state in the List instead of the App component. If you don't know, sort the list by "Title" and search for other stories afterward. What would be different if the sort state would be in the App component.
- Use your styling skills to give the user feedback about the current active sort and its reverse state. It could be an arrow up or arrow down SVG next to each active sort button.
- Optional: Leave feedback for this section[333].

---

[330]https://mzl.la/2XuN651
[331]https://bit.ly/3S3Do1C
[332]https://bit.ly/490Eimw
[333]https://forms.gle/ZoJSHFJf2swcBHXM6

Remember Last Searches

Task: Remember the last five search terms which hit the API, and provide a button to move quickly between searches. When the buttons are clicked, stories for the search term should be fetched again.

Optional Hints:

- Don't use a new state for this feature. Instead, reuse the url state and setUrl state updater function to fetch stories from the API. Adapt them to multiple urls as state, and to set multiple urls with setUrls. The last URL from urls can be used to fetch the data, and the last five URLs from urls can be used to display the buttons.

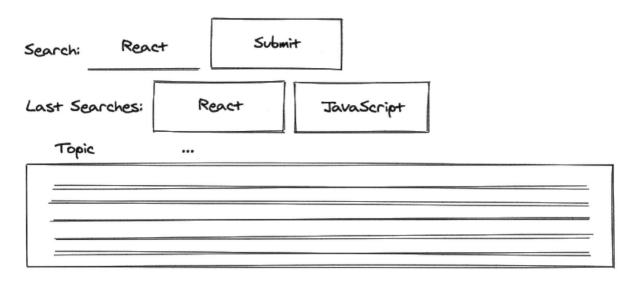

Let's get to it. First, we will refactor all url to urls state and all setUrl to setUrls state updater functions. Instead of initializing the state with an url as a string, make it an array with the initial url as its only entry:

src/App.jsx

```
const App = () => {
  ...

  const [urls, setUrls] = React.useState([
    `${API_ENDPOINT}${searchTerm}`,
  ]);

  ...
};
```

Second, instead of using the current url state for data fetching, use the last url entry from the urls array. If another url is added to the list of urls, it is used to fetch data instead:

src/App.jsx

```
const App = () => {

  ...

  const handleFetchStories = React.useCallback(async () => {
    dispatchStories({ type: 'STORIES_FETCH_INIT' });

    try {
      const lastUrl = urls[urls.length - 1];
      const result = await axios.get(lastUrl);

      dispatchStories({
        type: 'STORIES_FETCH_SUCCESS',
        payload: result.data.hits,
      });
    } catch {
      dispatchStories({ type: 'STORIES_FETCH_FAILURE' });
    }
  }, [urls]);

  ...

};
```

And third, instead of storing the url string as state with the state updater function, concatenate the new url using the concat method with the previous urls in an array for the new state:

src/App.jsx

```
const App = () => {
  ...

  const handleSearchSubmit = (event) => {
    const url = `${API_ENDPOINT}${searchTerm}`;
    setUrls(urls.concat(url));

    event.preventDefault();
  };

  ...

};
```

With each search, another URL is stored in our state of `urls`. Next, render a button for each of the last five URLs. We'll include a new universal handler for these buttons, and each passes a specific `url` with a more specific inline handler:

src/App.jsx

```
const getLastSearches = (urls) => urls.slice(-5);

...

const App = () => {
  ...

  const handleLastSearch = (url) => {
    // do something
  };

  const lastSearches = getLastSearches(urls);

  return (
    <div>
      <h1>My Hacker Stories</h1>

      <SearchForm ... />

      {lastSearches.map((url) => (
        <button
          key={url}
          type="button"
          onClick={() => handleLastSearch(url)}
        >
          {url}
        </button>
      ))}

      ...
    </div>
  );
};
```

Next, instead of showing the whole URL of the last search in the button as button text, show only the search term by replacing the API's endpoint with an empty string:

src/App.jsx

```
const extractSearchTerm = (url) => url.replace(API_ENDPOINT, '');

const getLastSearches = (urls) =>
  urls.slice(-5).map((url) => extractSearchTerm(url));

...

const App = () => {
  ...

  const lastSearches = getLastSearches(urls);

  return (
    <div>
      ...

      {lastSearches.map((searchTerm) => (
        <button
          key={searchTerm}
          type="button"
          onClick={() => handleLastSearch(searchTerm)}
        >
          {searchTerm}
        </button>
      ))}

      ...
    </div>
  );
};
```

The getLastSearches function now returns search terms instead of URLs. The actual searchTerm is passed to the inline handler instead of the url. By mapping over the list of urls in getLastSearches, we can extract the search term for each url within the array's map method. Making it more concise, it can also look like this:

src/App.jsx

```
const getLastSearches = (urls) =>
  urls.slice(-5).map(extractSearchTerm);
```

Now we'll provide functionality for the new handler used by every button, since clicking one of these buttons should trigger another search. Since we use the urls state for fetching data, and since we know the last URL is always used for data fetching, concatenate a new url to the list of urls to trigger another search request:

src/App.jsx

```
const App = () => {
  ...

  const handleLastSearch = (searchTerm) => {
    const url = `${API_ENDPOINT}${searchTerm}`;
    setUrls(urls.concat(url));
  };

  ...
};
```

If you compare this new handler's implementation logic to the handleSearchSubmit, you may see some common functionality. Extract this common functionality to a new handler and a new extracted utility function:

src/App.jsx

```
const getUrl = (searchTerm) => `${API_ENDPOINT}${searchTerm}`;

...

const App = () => {
  ...

  const handleSearch = (searchTerm) => {
    const url = getUrl(searchTerm);
    setUrls(urls.concat(url));
  };

  const handleSearchSubmit = (event) => {
    handleSearch(searchTerm);
```

```
    event.preventDefault();
  };

  const handleLastSearch = (searchTerm) => {
    handleSearch(searchTerm);
  };


  ...
};
```

The new utility function can be used somewhere else in the App component. If you extract functionality that can be used by two parties, always check to see if it can be used by a third-party:

src/App.jsx

```
const App = () => {
  ...


  // important: still wraps the returned value in []
  const [urls, setUrls] = React.useState([getUrl(searchTerm)]);


  ...
};
```

The functionality should work, but it complains or breaks if the same search term is used more than once, because searchTerm is used for each button element as key attribute. Make the key more specific by concatenating it with the index of the mapped array.

src/App.jsx

```
const App = () => {
  ...

  return (
    <div>
      ...

      {lastSearches.map((searchTerm, index) => (
        <button
          key={searchTerm + index}
          type="button"
          onClick={() => handleLastSearch(searchTerm)}
        >
          {searchTerm}
```

```
            </button>
        ))}


        ...
      </div>
    );
};
```

It's not the perfect solution, because the `index` isn't a stable key (especially when adding items to the list); however, it doesn't break in this scenario. The feature works now, but you can add further UX improvements by following the tasks below.

More Tasks:

- (1) Do not show the current search as a button, only the five preceding searches. Hint: Adapt the `getLastSearches` function.
- (2) Don't show duplicated searches. Searching twice for "React" shouldn't create two different buttons. Hint: Adapt the `getLastSearches` function.
- (3) Set the SearchForm component's input field value with the last search term if one of the buttons is clicked.

The source of the five rendered buttons is the `getLastSearches` function. There, we take the array of `urls` and return the last five entries from it. Now we'll change this utility function to return the last six entries instead of five by removing the last one, in order to not show the current search as a button. Afterward, only the five *previous* searches are displayed as buttons:

src/App.jsx

```
const getLastSearches = (urls) =>
  urls
    .slice(-6)
    .slice(0, -1)
    .map(extractSearchTerm);
```

If the same search is executed two or more times in a row, duplicate buttons appear, which is likely not your desired behavior. It would be acceptable to group identical searches into one button if they followed each other. We will solve this problem in the utility function as well. Before separating the array into the five previous searches, group the identical searches:

src/App.jsx

```
const getLastSearches = (urls) =>
  urls
    .reduce((result, url, index) => {
      const searchTerm = extractSearchTerm(url);

      if (index === 0) {
        return result.concat(searchTerm);
      }

      const previousSearchTerm = result[result.length - 1];

      if (searchTerm === previousSearchTerm) {
        return result;
      } else {
        return result.concat(searchTerm);
      }
    }, [])
    .slice(-6)
    .slice(0, -1);
```

The reduce function starts with an empty array as its result. The first iteration concatenates the searchTerm we extracted from the first url into the result. Every extracted searchTerm is compared to the one before it. If the previous search term is different from the current, concatenate the searchTerm to the result. If the search terms are identical, return the result without adding anything.

The SearchForm component's input field should be set with the new searchTerm if one of the last search buttons is clicked. We can solve this using the state updater function for the specific value used in the SearchForm component.

src/App.jsx

```
const App = () => {
  ...

  const handleLastSearch = (searchTerm) => {
    setSearchTerm(searchTerm);

    handleSearch(searchTerm);
  };

  ...
};
```

Lastly, extract the feature's new rendered content from this section as a standalone component, to keep the App component lightweight:

src/App.jsx

```
const App = () => {

  ...

  const lastSearches = getLastSearches(urls);

  return (
    <div>

      ...

      <SearchForm ... />

      <LastSearches
        lastSearches={lastSearches}
        onLastSearch={handleLastSearch}
      />

      <hr />

      ...
    </div>
  );
};

const LastSearches = ({ lastSearches, onLastSearch }) => (
  <>
    {lastSearches.map((searchTerm, index) => (
      <button
        key={searchTerm + index}
        type="button"
        onClick={() => onLastSearch(searchTerm)}
      >
        {searchTerm}
      </button>
    ))}
  </>
);
```

This feature wasn't an easy one. Lots of fundamental React but also JavaScript knowledge was needed to accomplish it. If you had no problems implementing it yourself or in following the instructions, you are very well set. If you had one or the other issue, don't worry too much about it. Maybe you even figured out another way to solve this task and it may have turned out simpler than the one I showed here.

Exercises:

- Compare your source code against the author's source code[334].
    - Recap all the source code changes from this section[335].
- Read more about grouping in JavaScript[336].
- Optional: Leave feedback for this section[337].

---

[334]https://bit.ly/3SmzaDJ
[335]https://bit.ly/48Jyuhp
[336]https://www.robinwieruch.de/javascript-groupby/
[337]https://forms.gle/LhNVodZgu8qTqHhN6

Paginated Fetch

Searching for popular stories via Hacker News API is only one step towards a fully functional search engine, and there are many ways to fine-tune the search. Take a closer look at the data structure and observe how the Hacker News API[338] returns more than a list of `hits`. Specifically, it returns a paginated list. The page property, which is 0 in the first response, can be used to fetch more paginated lists as results. You only need to pass the next page with the same search term to the API.

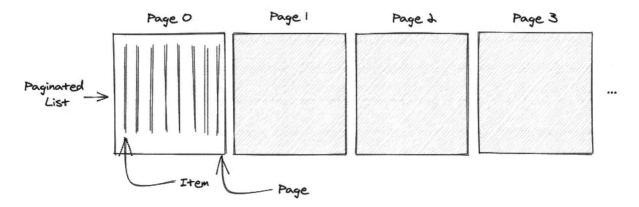

The following shows how to implement a paginated fetch with the Hacker News data structure. If you are used to **pagination** from other applications, you may have a row of buttons from 1-10 in your mind – where the currently selected page is highlighted 1-[3]-10 and where clicking one of the buttons leads to fetching and displaying this subset of data.

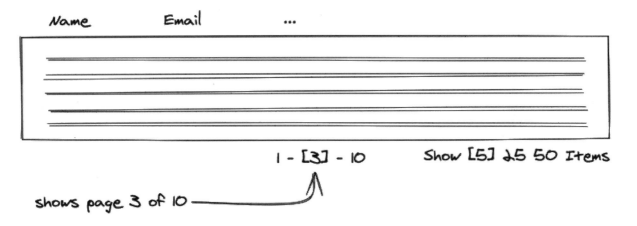

In contrast, we will implement the feature as **infinite pagination**. Instead of rendering a single paginated list on a button click, we will render *all paginated lists as one list* with *one* button to fetch the next page. Every additional *paginated list* is concatenated at the end of the *one list*.

---

[338]https://hn.algolia.com/api

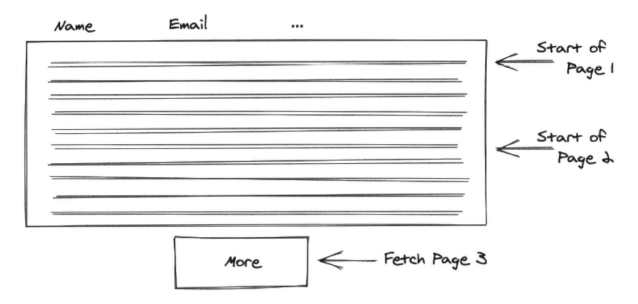

Task: Rather than fetching only the first page of a list, extend the functionality for fetching succeeding pages. Implement this as infinite pagination on button click.

Optional Hints:

- Extend the API_ENDPOINT with the parameters needed for the paginated fetch.
- Store the page from the result as state after fetching the data.
- Fetch the first page (0) of data with every search.
- Fetch the succeeding page (page + 1) for every additional request triggered with a new HTML button.

Let's do this! First, extend the API constant so it can deal with paginated data later. We will turn this one constant:

src/App.jsx

```
const API_ENDPOINT = 'https://hn.algolia.com/api/v1/search?query=';

const getUrl = (searchTerm) => `${API_ENDPOINT}${searchTerm}`;
```

Into a composable API constant with its parameters:

src/App.jsx

```
const API_BASE = 'https://hn.algolia.com/api/v1';
const API_SEARCH = '/search';
const PARAM_SEARCH = 'query=';

// careful: notice the ? in between
const getUrl = (searchTerm) =>
  `${API_BASE}${API_SEARCH}?${PARAM_SEARCH}${searchTerm}`;
```

Fortunately, we don't need to adjust the API endpoints at other places of the application, because we extracted a common getUrl function for it. However, there is one spot where we must address this logic for the future:

src/App.jsx

```
const extractSearchTerm = (url) => url.replace(API_ENDPOINT, '');
```

In the next steps, it won't be sufficient to replace the base of our API endpoint, which is no longer in our code. With more parameters for the API endpoint, the URL becomes more complex. It will change from X to Y:

src/App.jsx

```
// X
https://hn.algolia.com/api/v1/search?query=react

// Y
https://hn.algolia.com/api/v1/search?query=react&page=0
```

It's better to extract the search term by extracting everything between ? and &. Also consider that the query parameter is directly after the ? and all other parameters like page follow it:

src/App.jsx

```
const extractSearchTerm = (url) =>
  url.substring(url.lastIndexOf('?') + 1, url.lastIndexOf('&'));
```

The key (query=) also needs to be replaced, leaving only the value (searchTerm):

src/App.jsx

```
const extractSearchTerm = (url) =>
  url
    .substring(url.lastIndexOf('?') + 1, url.lastIndexOf('&'))
    .replace(PARAM_SEARCH, '');
```

Essentially, we'll trim the string until we leave only the search term:

src/App.jsx

```
// url
https://hn.algolia.com/api/v1/search?query=react&page=0

// url after substring
query=react

// url after replace
react
```

Next, the returned result from the Hacker News API delivers us the page data:

src/App.jsx

```
const App = () => {
  ...

  const handleFetchStories = React.useCallback(async () => {
    dispatchStories({ type: 'STORIES_FETCH_INIT' });

    try {
      const lastUrl = urls[urls.length - 1];
      const result = await axios.get(lastUrl);

      dispatchStories({
        type: 'STORIES_FETCH_SUCCESS',
        payload: {
          list: result.data.hits,
          page: result.data.page,
        },
      });
    } catch {
      dispatchStories({ type: 'STORIES_FETCH_FAILURE' });
    }
  }, [urls]);
```

```
  ...
};
```

We need to store this data to make paginated fetches later:

src/App.jsx

```
const storiesReducer = (state, action) => {
  switch (action.type) {
    case 'STORIES_FETCH_INIT':
      ...
    case 'STORIES_FETCH_SUCCESS':
      return {
        ...state,
        isLoading: false,
        isError: false,
        data: action.payload.list,
        page: action.payload.page,
      };
    case 'STORIES_FETCH_FAILURE':
      ...
    case 'REMOVE_STORY':
      ...
    default:
      throw new Error();
  }
};

const App = () => {
  ...

  const [stories, dispatchStories] = React.useReducer(
    storiesReducer,
    { data: [], page: 0, isLoading: false, isError: false }
  );

  ...
};
```

Extend the API endpoint with the new page parameter. This change was supported by our premature optimizations earlier, when we extracted the search term from the URL:

src/App.jsx

```
const API_BASE = 'https://hn.algolia.com/api/v1';
const API_SEARCH = '/search';
const PARAM_SEARCH = 'query=';
const PARAM_PAGE = 'page=';

// careful: notice the ? and & in between
const getUrl = (searchTerm, page) =>
  `${API_BASE}${API_SEARCH}?${PARAM_SEARCH}${searchTerm}&${PARAM_PAGE}${page}`;
```

Next, we must adjust all getUrl invocations by passing the page argument. Since the initial search and the last search always fetch the first page (0), we pass this page as an argument to the function for retrieving the appropriate URL:

src/App.jsx

```
const App = () => {
  ...

  const [urls, setUrls] = React.useState([getUrl(searchTerm, 0)]);

  ...

  const handleSearch = (searchTerm, page) => {
    const url = getUrl(searchTerm, page);
    setUrls(urls.concat(url));
  };

  const handleSearchSubmit = (event) => {
    handleSearch(searchTerm, 0);

    event.preventDefault();
  };

  const handleLastSearch = (searchTerm) => {
    setSearchTerm(searchTerm);

    handleSearch(searchTerm, 0);
  };

  ...
};
```

To fetch the next page when a button is clicked, we'll need to increment the page argument in this new handler:

src/App.jsx

```
const App = () => {
  ...

  const handleMore = () => {
    const lastUrl = urls[urls.length - 1];
    const searchTerm = extractSearchTerm(lastUrl);
    handleSearch(searchTerm, stories.page + 1);
  };

  ...

  return (
    <div>
      ...

      {stories.isLoading ? (
        <p>Loading ...</p>
      ) : (
        <List list={stories.data} onRemoveItem={handleRemoveStory} />
      )}

      <button type="button" onClick={handleMore}>
        More
      </button>
    </div>
  );
};
```

We've implemented data fetching with the dynamic page argument. The initial and last searches always use the first page, and every fetch with the new "More"-button uses an incremented page. There is one crucial bug when trying the feature, though: the new fetches don't extend the previous list, but completely replace it.

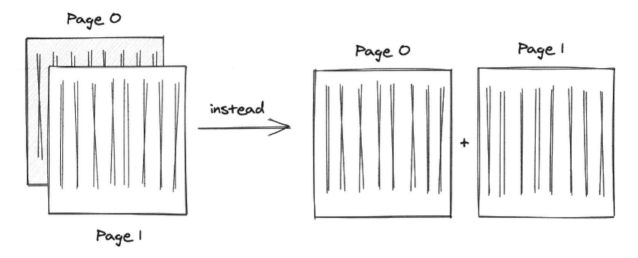

We solve this in the reducer by avoiding the replacement of current data with new data, concate-nating the paginated lists:

src/App.jsx

```
const storiesReducer = (state, action) => {
  switch (action.type) {
    case 'STORIES_FETCH_INIT':
      ...
    case 'STORIES_FETCH_SUCCESS':
      return {
        ...state,
        isLoading: false,
        isError: false,
        data:
          action.payload.page === 0
            ? action.payload.list
            : state.data.concat(action.payload.list),
        page: action.payload.page,
      };
    case 'STORIES_FETCH_FAILURE':
      ...
    case 'REMOVE_STORY':
      ...
    default:
      throw new Error();
  }
};
```

The displayed list grows after fetching more data with the new button. However, there is still a flicker straining the UX. When fetching paginated data, the list disappears for a moment because the loading indicator appears and reappears after the request resolves.

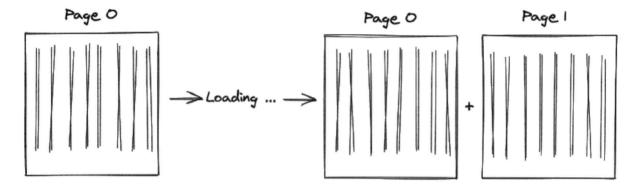

The desired behavior is to render the list – which is an empty list in the beginning – and replace the "More"-button with the loading indicator only for the next requests. This is a common UI refactoring for conditional rendering when the task evolves from a single list to paginated lists:

src/App.jsx

```
const App = () => {
  ...

  return (
    <div>
      ...

      <List list={stories.data} onRemoveItem={handleRemoveStory} />

      {stories.isLoading ? (
        <p>Loading ...</p>
      ) : (
        <button type="button" onClick={handleMore}>
          More
        </button>
      )}
    </div>
  );
};
```

It's possible to fetch ongoing data for popular stories now. When working with third-party APIs, it's always a good idea to explore its API surface. Every remote API returns different data structures, so its features may vary.

Exercises:

- Compare your source code against the author's source code[339].
  - Recap all the source code changes from this section[340].
- Revisit the Hacker News API documentation[341]: Is there a way to fetch more items in a list for a page by just adding further parameters to the API endpoint?
- Revisit the beginning of this section which speaks about pagination and infinite pagination. How would you implement a normal pagination component with buttons from 1-[3]-10, where each button fetches and displays only one page of the list?
- Instead of having one "More"-button, how would you implement infinite pagination with an infinite scroll technique? Rather than clicking a button for fetching the next page explicitly, the infinite scroll could fetch the next page once the viewport of the browser hits the bottom of the displayed list.
- Optional: Leave feedback for this section[342].

---

[339]https://bit.ly/3HvbI0A
[340]https://bit.ly/3SpLtiH
[341]https://hn.algolia.com/api
[342]https://forms.gle/maPsfzHLba8gheCQA

Deploying a React Application

Now it's time to get out into the world with your React application. There are many ways to deploy a React application to production, and many competing providers that offer this service. We'll keep it simple here by narrowing it down on one provider, after which you'll be equipped to check out other hosting providers on your own.

Build Process

So far, everything we've done has been the *development stage* of the application, when the development server handles everything: packaging all files to one application and serving it on localhost on your local machine. As a result, our code isn't available for anyone else.

The next step is to take your application to the *production stage* by hosting it on a remote server, called deployment, making it accessible for users of your application. Before an application can go public, it needs to be packaged as one essential application. Redundant code, testing code, and duplications are removed. There is also a process called minification at work which reduces the code size once more.

Fortunately, optimizations and packaging, also called bundling, comes with the build tools in Vite. First, build your application on the command line:

Command Line

```
npm run build
```

This creates a new *dist/* folder in your project with the bundled application. You could take this folder and deploy it on a hosting provider now, but we'll use a local server to mimic this process before engaging in the real thing. On the command line, serve your application with this Vite's local HTTP server:

Command Line

```
npm run preview
```

A URL is presented that provides access to your optimized, packaged and hosted application. It's sent through a local IP address that can be made available over your local network, meaning we're hosting the application on our local machine.

Exercises:

- Optional: Leave feedback for this section[343].

---

[343]https://forms.gle/hFsut8q7eYsWfYL7A

Deploy to Firebase

After we've built a full-fledged application in React, the final step is deployment. It is the tipping point of getting your ideas into the world, from learning how to code to producing applications. We will use Firebase Hosting for deployment.

Firebase works for React, as well as most libraries and frameworks like Angular and Vue. First, install the Firebase CLI globally to the node modules:

Command Line

```
npm install -g firebase-tools
```

Using a global installation of the Firebase CLI lets us deploy applications without concern over project dependency. For any globally-installed node package, remember to update it to a newer version with the same command whenever needed:

Command Line

```
npm install -g firebase-tools
```

If you don't have a Firebase project yet, sign up for a Firebase account[344] and create a new project there. Then you can associate the Firebase CLI with the Firebase account (Google account):

Command Line

```
firebase login
```

A URL will display on the command line that you can open in a browser, or the Firebase CLI opens it. Choose a Google account to create a Firebase project, and give Google the necessary permissions. Return to the command line to verify a successful login. Next, move to the project's folder and execute the following command, which initializes a Firebase project for the Firebase hosting features:

Command Line

```
firebase init
```

Then choose the Hosting option. If you're interested in using another tool next to Firebase Hosting, add other options:

---

[344]https://console.firebase.google.com

Command Line

```
? Which Firebase features do you want to set up for this directory?
 ☐ Firestore: Configure security rules and indexes files for Firestore
 ☐ Functions: Configure a Cloud Functions directory and its files
 ☐☐ Hosting: Configure files for Firebase Hosting ...
 ☐ Hosting: Set up GitHub Action deploys
 ☐ Storage: Configure a security rules file for Cloud Storage
```

Google becomes aware of all Firebase projects associated with an account after login. However, for this project we will start with a new project on the Firebase platform:

Command Line

```
First, let's associate this project directory with a Firebase project.
You can create multiple project aliases by running firebase use --add,
but for now we'll just set up a default project.

? Please select an option:
  Use an existing project
☐ Create a new project
  Add Firebase to an existing Google Cloud Platform project
  Don't set up a default project
```

There are a few other configuration steps to define. Instead of using the default *public/* folder, we want to use the *dist/* folder from Vite. Alternatively if you set up the bundling with a tool like Webpack yourself, you can choose the appropriate name for the build folder:

Command Line

```
? What do you want to use as your public directory? dist
? Configure as a single-page app (rewrite all urls to /index.html)? Yes
? Set up automatic builds and deploys with GitHub? No
☐  Wrote dist/index.html
```

The Vite application creates a *dist/* folder after we perform the npm run build for the first time. The folder contains all the merged content from the *public/* folder and the *src/* folder. Since it is a single page application, we want to redirect the user to the *index.html* file, so the React router can handle client-side routing.

Now your Firebase initialization is complete. This step created a few configuration files for Firebase Hosting in your project's folder. You can read more about them in Firebase's documentation[345] for configuring redirects, a 404 page, or headers. Finally, deploy your React application with Firebase on the command line:

---

[345]https://bit.ly/3DVgbpG

Command Line

```
firebase deploy
```

After a successful deployment, you should see a similar output with your project's identifier:

Command Line

```
Project Console: https://console.firebase.google.com/project/my-react-project-abc123\
/overview
Hosting URL: https://my-react-project-abc123.firebaseapp.com
```

Visit both pages to observe the results. The first link navigates to your Firebase project's dashboard, where you'll see a new panel for the Firebase Hosting. The second link navigates to your deployed React application.

If you see a blank page for your deployed React application, make sure the public key/value pair in the *firebase.json* is set to dist (or whichever name you chose for this folder). Second, verify you've run the build script for your React app with npm run build. Finally, check out the official troubleshoot area for deploying Vite applications to Firebase[346]. Try another deployment with firebase deploy.

Exercises:

- Read more about Firebase Hosting[347].
  - Connect your domain to your Firebase deployed application[348].
- Optional: If you want to have a managed cloud server, check out DigitalOcean[349]. It's more work, but it allows more control. I host all my websites, web applications, and backend APIs there[350].
- Optional: Leave feedback for this section[351].

---

[346]https://bit.ly/3Sp2Xsn
[347]https://bit.ly/3lXypAC
[348]https://bit.ly/3phFxdp
[349]https://m.do.co/c/fb27c90322f3
[350]https://www.robinwieruch.de/deploy-applications-digital-ocean/
[351]https://forms.gle/QPjydK8UbaXkxCEj9

Outline

We've reached the end of the Road to React, and I hope you enjoyed reading it, and that it helped you gain traction in React. If you liked the book, share it with your friends who are interested in learning more about React. Also, a review on Amazon[352] or Goodreads[353] would be very much appreciated.

From here, I recommend you extend the application to create your own React projects before engaging another book, course, or tutorial. Try it for a week, take it to production by deploying it, and reach out to me or others to showcase it. I am always interested in seeing what my readers built, and learning how I can help them along.

If you're looking for extensions for your application, I recommend several learning paths after you've mastered the fundamentals:

- **Routing**: You can implement routing for your application with React Router[354]. There is only one page in the application we've created, but that will grow. React Router helps manage multiple pages across multiple URLs. When you introduce routing to your application, no requests are made to the web server for the next page. The router handles this client-side.
- **Connecting to a Database and/or Authentication**: Growing React applications will eventually require persistent data. The data should be stored in a database so that keeps it intact after browser sessions, to be shared with different users. Firebase is one of the simplest ways to introduce a database without writing a backend application. In my book titled "The Road to Firebase"[355], you will find a step-by-step guide on how to use Firebase authentication and database in React.
- **Connecting to a Backend**: React handles frontend applications, and we've only requested data from a third-party backend's API thus far. You can also introduce an API with a backend application that connects to a database and manages authentication/authorization. In "The Road to GraphQL"[356], I teach you how to use GraphQL for client-server communication. You'll learn how to connect your backend to a database, how to manage user sessions, and how to talk from a frontend to your backend application via a GraphQL API.
- **State Management**: You have used React to manage local component state exclusively in this learning experience. It's a good start for most applications, but there are also external state management solutions for React. I explore the most popular one in my book "The Road to Redux"[357].

---

[352]https://amzn.to/2JHlP42

[353]https://www.goodreads.com/book/show/37503118-the-road-to-learn-react

[354]https://www.robinwieruch.de/react-router/

[355]https://www.roadtofirebase.com/

[356]https://www.roadtographql.com/

[357]https://www.roadtoredux.com/

- **Tooling with Webpack and Babel:** We used *Vite* to set up the application in this book. At some point you may want to learn the tooling around it, to create projects without *Vite*. I recommend a minimal setup with Webpack[358], after which you can apply additional tooling.
- **Code Organization:** Recall the chapter about code organization and apply these changes, if you haven't already. It will help organize your components into structured files and folders, and it will help you understand the principles of code splitting, reusability, maintainability, and module API design. Your application will grow and need structured modules eventually; so it's better to start now.
- **Testing:** We only scratched the surface of testing. If you are unfamiliar with testing web applications, dive deeper into unit testing and integration testing[359], especially with React Testing Library for unit/integration testing and Cypress for end-to-end testing in React.
- **Type Checking:** Earlier we used TypeScript in React, which is good practice to prevent bugs and improve the developer experience. Dive deeper into this topic to make your JavaScript applications more robust. Maybe you'll end up using TypeScript instead of JavaScript all along.
- **UI Components:** Many beginners introduce UI component libraries like Material UI too early in their projects. It is more practical to use a dropdown, checkbox, or dialog in React with standard HTML elements. Most of these components will manage their own local state. A checkbox has to know whether it is checked or unchecked, so you should implement them as controlled components. After you cover the basic implementations of these crucial UI components, introducing a UI component library should become easier.
- **React Native:** React Native[360] brings your application to mobile devices like iOS and Android. Once you've mastered React, the learning curve for React Native shouldn't be that steep, as they share the same principles. The only difference with mobile devices are the layout components, the build tools, and the APIs of your mobile device.

I invite you to visit my website[361] to find more interesting topics about web development and software engineering. You can also subscribe to my Newsletter[362] or Twitter page[363] to get updates about articles, books, and courses. If you have only the book and want to extend it to the course, check out the official course website[364].

Thank you for reading the Road to React.

Regards,

Robin Wieruch

[358]https://www.robinwieruch.de/minimal-react-webpack-babel-setup/
[359]https://www.robinwieruch.de/react-testing-tutorial/
[360]https://facebook.github.io/react-native/
[361]https://www.robinwieruch.de
[362]https://rwieruch.substack.com/
[363]https://twitter.com/rwieruch
[364]https://www.roadtoreact.com/